A DICTIONARY OF DEVON DIALECT

A DICTIONARY OF DEVON DIALECT

John Downes

TABB HOUSE

© John Downes 1986

Typeset by St George Printing Works Ltd, 1-3-5 Wesley Street, Camborne, Cornwall.
Printed and bound in Great Britain by A. Wheaton & Co., Exeter

First published 1986
Tabb House, 11 Church Street, Padstow, Cornwall, PL28 8BG

CONTENTS

PUBLISHER'S NOTE

Apostrophes to denote the omission of letters, as used in the spelling of standard English, have been omitted in most cases from dialect spellings, except to indicate pronunciation where a slight hesitation in the speaking of a word gives it a diphthong. Thus taw'd, or tow'd, which could be spelt phonetically as towad.

ACKNOWLEDGMENTS

IT would be inappropriate for me to attempt to publish this book without acknowledging the help and encouragement I have received.

Although I cannot mention all those who have contributed, indeed I do not know who many of them are or were, I can thank E. W. Martin Esq., FR HIST.S, author and critic, whose kindly advice and scholarship have been of enormous help to me.

There have been many others who have helped, including the late Ernest T. Abel Esq., MA, the Recorder of Dialect for the Devonshire Association, who sadly did not live to see the publication of this book. But above all I owe my thanks to my secretary, Mrs Kaye Phillips, who has typed, re-typed, corrected and re-corrected the typescript with never a complaint, and to my wife who has put up with the book, and the chaos it has caused in our household for many years.

Notwithstanding the assistance which I have received, the opinions expressed are my own, and any errors and omissions are my responsibility.

John Downes
Woolfardisworthy, Bideford
1986

INTRODUCTION

THIS book has taken a very long time to write and even longer to check and to cross-check. Having at last finished, perhaps the most difficult task is to know what to call it! Is it indeed a dictionary? I certainly would never have dared set out to write one, and yet the Oxford English Dictionary (after this referred to as the OED), defines a dictionary as:

A book dealing with the words of a language, so as to set forth their orthography, pronunciation, signification, and use, their synonyms, derivation, and history, or at least some of these; the words are arranged in some stated order, now, usually, alphabetical; a word-book, vocabulary, lexicon.

By definition then, it must be at least partly a dictionary, but if I did not set out to write a dictionary what then was my objective?

Between 1950 and 1962 a survey of English dialects was made by the Department of English Language and Medieval English Literature at Leeds University. Planned in 1946, this survey grew from a proposal made by Professor Dieth of the University of Zurich that he and Professor Harold Orton of Leeds should together compile a 'linguistic atlas' of England. Unfortunately Professor Dieth died in 1956 before the work was completed.

The Leeds Survey, which must be respected by all scholars of the English language, consists of twelve volumes, covers all English dialects and is a very detailed and academic work. However, it was clearly never intended for the general reader and my aim has simply been to provide a book that is.

Whilst there has long been an interest in dialect, there is

considerable misunderstanding about what the word means. Many people seem to confuse it with regional accents and when they call for dialect to be preserved or even taught in schools, they are probably thinking more of regional accent than of dialect.

That these accents are a part of dialect is unarguable, but there are many people who speak with regional accents who know few true dialect words, and the number of people who use genuine dialect in normal conversation is decreasing and will continue to decrease.

The definition of dialect is interesting and complex. The OED says that dialect is:

Manner of speaking, language, speech; *esp.* one peculiar to an individual or class; phraseology, idiom... A variety of a language arising from local peculiarities... A variety of speech differing from the standard language; a provincial method of speech.

This definition covers a great deal of ground, but I believe that dialect contains at least six different ingredients which mix together to make a diverse and fascinating whole. They are

   a. local pronunciation,
   b. regional accents (related to pronun-
      ciation),
   c. grammatical construction which differs from that which is generally accepted as being correct,
   d. unusual use of standard words,
   e. the deliberate or accidental mis-use of standard words, and
   f. the use of archaic words in normal conversation.

Evidence suggest that regional dialects were once widely spoken by all social classes. Trevelyan says that in Queen Anne's time the country squire spoke in a broad provincial dialect and was only distinguished from the yeoman by the respect paid to him by others. This situation did not last.

During the seventeenth and eighteenth centuries there appears to have been a widespread desire to purify languages. Academics had for a long time regarded Latin as being the only model for language and literature and many had attempted to refine English on Latin lines. It is obvious that standardisation of both grammar and spelling was highly desirable for the spelling of the same words often differed from line to line. Edward VI's prayerbook, introduced in 1549 but still in daily use in the first half of the seventeenth century, provides many examples:

O ye waters that be aboue the fyrmamente, speake good of the *Lorde* prayse hym, and set hym up for euer
O all ye powers of the *Lord,* speake good of the *Lord.* . .

In the prayer-book the words *Catholic faith* are spelled *Catholyke fayth* in one line and, three lines later, *Catholike faith.* Even a simple word like *him* varied, being spelled as it is now in one line and *hym* in the next. There was a desire for uniformity, but no standard to which one could refer.

Shakespeare could not even decide how to spell his own name. It ranged from *Chacksper* to *Shaxpere,* from *Shakespere* or *Shakespeyre* to *Schakespeire* and even *Schakspere,* and there were other variations. He invented words of his own; some survive only in his works and have not been used by anyone else. But some of the words which he coined have become part of the English language and include such commonplace words as *accommodation, dislocate, premeditate* and *submerge.* Another word which he almost certainly invented is *auspicious* (or rather, *inauspicious*), and this word seems to have arrived on the stage when Romeo says, just before he commits suicide,

> . . . here, will I remain
> With worms that are thy chambermaids: O here
> Will I set up my everlasting rest;
> And shake the yoke of *inauspicious* stars
> From this world-wearied flesh. Eyes, look
> your last!...

He obtained the word from the Latin *auspex* (someone who looked for omens in the flight of birds.)

The first English dictionary I know of was a book of 120 pages written by Robert Cawdrey in 1604 called *The Table Alphabeticall of Hard Words*. This was followed in 1616, the year of Shakespeare's death, by John Bullokar's *English Expositor,* and a book called *A Guide Into Tongues* appeared in 1617.

Cockeram published his *English Dictionarie: or an Interpreter of Hard English Words* in 1623, but this, like earlier works, was merely a list of difficult words with no attempt to provide etymology or examples of usage.

In 1658 Milton's nephew Edward Phillips produced a book called *A New World of English Words*. This was followed in 1721 by the publication of Bailey's *Universal Etymological English Dictionary* but even the improved edition which was not published until 1736 was inferior to works produced on their respective languages by academies in Italy and in France.

The desire to codify and purify language was not confined to England and the Accademia della Crusca had been founded as long ago as 1582 to purify the Italian language. In 1635, Cardinal Richelieu had been responsible for the foundation of a society which came to be known as the Académie Français and its function was to give definite rulings on the French language.

In 1712 Jonathan Swift addressed a letter to the Earl of Oxford, the Lord Treasurer of England, proposing that certain suitable persons should assemble to produce rules to codify the English language.

Nothing came of this, principally because of the death of Queen Anne, for the Lord Treasurer had hoped to use his influence with the Queen to obtain funds from which the cost could be met. Swift had, in effect, proposed the formation of an academy similar to those already existing in Italy and in France, but many, including Dr Johnson, opposed it. He hoped that 'the spirit of English liberty' would hinder or destroy the establishment of such an institution. When his dictionary was published in 1755 Dr Johnson established a standard which remained unchallenged for almost one hundred years.

As this seventeenth and eighteenth century cultural revolution was taking place the social structure of the countryside was undergoing change. Land values almost doubled between 1700 and 1790 and more and more land was brought into cultivation. Better farming methods were introduced and experiments were made with crop rotation. These new methods required land to be enclosed and the procedure used to achieve this was usually by an act of Parliament and seldom by voluntary agreement.

Between 1760 and 1801 more than 1,300 enclosure acts were passed, and then a General Enclosure Act was introduced to make the enclosure of land simpler. By 1820 almost 1,000 more acts were passed and this transformed not only the appearance of the countryside but the lives of the rural working classes. It took away the independence of many small-holders who had kept their livestock on common land. An anonymous writer in the *Tickler Magazine* said on February 1st, 1821

> The fault is great in man or woman
> Who steals a goose from off a common;
> But what can plead that man's excuse
> Who steals a common from the goose?

When enclosed land became private property the formerly independent small farmer had no option but to become a farm labourer or go and seek work in the growing industrial towns.

Europe had been at war for many years and the transition to peace brought with it many problems. In 1825 William Cobbett claimed that taxation, the National Debt, the issue of paper money, and what he delighted to call 'The Thing', (meaning the system of Government which he so deplored), had contributed towards turning farm workers into paupers and separating them from the farmers and yeomen.

Cobbett claimed that it cost less to pay farm workers money and to house them in cottages than it had cost to board them in the farmer's own house. He speaks of this 'accursed system' which turned farmers into a 'species of mock gentlefolk, while it has ground the labourers down into real slaves.' He said that the squire's father

used to, I dare say, sit at the head of the oak table along with his men, say grace with them, and cut up the meat and the pudding. He might take a cup of strong beer to himself when they have none; but that was pretty nearly all the difference in their manner of living. . .

As a direct result of these social changes, it became the fashion for farmers and the new rural gentry to send their children away to school where they were taught to 'speak properly' and to read and learn the classics. The gap between the ploughboy and the farmer's son widened, and there developed a difference in their mode of speech. Ernest Martin says that the enclosures so upset the balance of rural life that many farmers found it difficult to determine their place in society. Some aped the squire simply because they no longer knew where they belonged.

A farmer in Berkshire, quoted by Lord Ernle, expressed the dominant social attitudes of two periods of village life:

1743	1843
Man, to the plough:	Man, Tally Ho!
Wife, to the cow;	Miss, Piano,
Girl, to the yarn;	Wife, Silk and Satin,
Boy, to the Barn;	Boy, Greek and Latin
And your Rent will	And you'll all be
be netted	Gazetted.

There is plenty of other evidence in contemporary literature of these changes and in *Persuasion* Jane Austen said

the Musgroves, like their houses, were in a state of alteration, perhaps improvement. The father and mother were in the old English style and the young people in the new. Mr and Mrs Musgrove were a very good sort of people; friendly and hospitable, not much educated, and not at all elegant. . . [their daughters] had brought from a school at Exeter all the usual stock of accomplishments, and were now, like thousands of other young ladies, living to be fashionable. . .

This upheaval in the pattern of country life and speech continued uninterrupted because until the introduction of the first Education Act in 1870 very few children of labourers received any education. They learned, as their fathers had learned before them, by word of mouth.

It was during this period that a few educated persons became interested in the traditional speech of the County and although the earliest example of recorded dialect is probably the 'Exmoor Scolding and Courtship', published in 1746, most interest seems to have come during the nineteenth century. In the early 1800s Mrs Palmer, a sister of Sir Joshua Reynolds, wrote a little story in Devon dialect. This was edited and published by her daughter, Mrs Gwatkin of Great Torrington, in 1839.

In 1866 Sir John Bowring, who became President of the Devonshire Association for the Advancement of Science, Literature and Art in 1862, presented a paper at

Tavistock on the subject of dialect saying

It is not a hazardous prophecy to announce that in a few generations no language but English, and that, a grammatical English, will be spoken throughout the British Territories. The old British is dead, the Gaelic will perish next, then the Welsh and last, probably Erse, or Irish, and then our Mother tongue, emphatically English, will be the sole sovereign over the whole dominions of our written and spoken literature. Education and fashion will cause the diversities of colloquial idioms to disappear. . .

Sir John then said 'Half a century ago, the county of a country gentleman was easily discoverable wherever he went; ''You are a Devonshire, a Yorkshire, a Kentishman'' frequently larded the conversation. . .'

In 1875 Frederick Thomas Elworthy, who became President of the Devonshire Association in 1906, read a paper before the Philological Society entitled 'The Dialect of West Somerset'. Elworthy said that the claim that the last trace of Briton, Saxon, and Dane would soon be swept out of the land by railways, telegraphs, machinery, and steam was highly coloured.

He believed that the introduction of modern improvements and the advance of science had far less effect on dialect than was generally supposed by those whose acquaintance with dialect was confined, in the most part, to what others had written. One cannot help wondering what he would have thought of the effects of radio and television. Nevertheless he was right, and one must turn again to Dr Johnson for the real reason. He said in the preface to his dictionary

As language was at its beginning merely oral, all words of necessary or common use were spoken before they were written; and while they were unfixed by any visible signs, must have been spoken with great diversity, as we now observe those who cannot read to catch sounds imperfectly and utter them negligently. When this wild and barbarous jargon was first reduced to an alphabet, every penman endeavoured to express, as he could, the sounds which he was accustomed to pronounce or to receive, and vitiated in writing such words as were already vitiated in speech. . . from this uncertain pronunciation arise in great part the various dialects of the same country, which will always be observed to grow fewer, and less different, as books are multiplied. . .

Dialect is not being destroyed or killed. It is simply dying of old age.

This is true of many things but while dialect is not an artifact that can be encased in plastic or preserved in a museum, unless it is recorded it will, sooner or later, be lost for ever.

This was the view of the Devonshire Association when in 1877 it appointed a committee to record what it called 'verbal provincialisms'. The regulations of that committee are not without interest. Members were urged

'To regard the following as Devonshire Provincialisms if used by a speaker or writer within Devonshire, irrespective of their being, or not being, used elsewhere:-

(a) Every word not occurring in a good English dictionary of the present day.

(b) Every word which, though occurring in any good English dictionary of the present day, is used in a sense differing from any definition used in such a dictionary.

(c) Every provincial pronunciation of such a word which is not in itself a provincialism.

(d) Every provincial phrase or expression.

(e) Every provincial name of an animal, vegetable or other object.'

There were ten regulations that required members to note where each provincialism was heard, or seen in writing, and to accept nothing second-hand. Members were required to state the sex, occupation, residence, birth-place, and age of the person using the provincialism.

The terms of reference suggest that dialect was being treated as something of a curiosity, the language of creatures living in a strange etymological zoo rather than as a living language, which, until relatively recently, had been in general use.

The committee dispersed in 1923 but since then the Devonshire Association has appointed a recorder of dialect whose report appears in the annual transactions of the Association. When the first recorder was appointed the rules and regulations were slightly modified but they remain substantially the same as the original ones.

R. Pearse Chope, who became the Association's President in 1926, read a paper before it in July 1891 and then published it under the title of 'The Dialect of Hartland, Devonshire'. The paper was originally prepared as a commentary on Elworthy's *The West Somerset Word Book*. He seems to have accepted that education and 'progress' was responsible for the gradual disappearance of dialect:

. . .it is obvious that the old words are retained longest where the progress is slowest; that is in those places which are furthest from the railways, because board schools and newspapers are now common to all.

Bideford is no longer connected with London by the railway and Hartland is now further from the railway than it was in 1891, but the trains have been replaced by motor cars which, with radio and television, bring 'progress' to all.

But although Bowring and Elworthy spoke of the approaching death of dialect and whilst a committee was created in 1877 to record dialect before it disappeared completely, it is still spoken by many people. Nevertheless it is still on its way out and one must ask why.

'What' demanded Dr Johnson, 'makes a word obsolete more than general agreement to forbear it?'

Dialect is disappearing because most people do not want to use it. But despite this, there is a genuine interest in dialect for its own sake, perhaps a nostalgia for the speech of the past and a reluctance to see yet another milestone of social history disappear for ever.

Sadly, mock dialect is now used to indicate the whereabouts of the public bar or the lavatories with signs like YER TIZ or UP YER. This sort of thing, plus what has so aptly been called on radio and television the Mummerset accent, and articles in magazines and newspapers which pretend to be dialect (but which are in fact stories written to convey to the uninitiated the impression of dialect), is all that many people know, or care, about the dying language of our county.

If this book succeeds in stimulating interest in the genuine dialect words of Devon, then I shall have achieved my object.

Chapter 1

ACCENT AND PRONUNCIATION

NO matter what method is used, it is not easy to record accent in writing. It is even more difficult to differentiate between accent and pronunciation. Was it, for example, pronunciation or accent which caused the downfall of the Ephraimites at the passage of Jordan? 'Say now Shibboleth: and he said Siboleth: for he could not frame to pronounce it right' (Judges XII. v.6) is surely one of the earliest references to this complex subject.

Most people can without difficulty recognise a so-called American accent, or a North Country or West Country accent. Americans even refer to a British accent but probably mean what used to be called an Oxford accent or one of the many regional accents which proclaim the speaker to be British.

In Shaw's *Pygmalion,* Professor Higgins, by listening to a person speak, is able to say where in London, within a few streets, the speaker comes from. Whilst this is far-fetched, accents can be used to identify a speaker's origins. The accent of a Bostonian differs from that of a Texan, that of a Lancastrian from that of a man from York and, to the informed ear, the accent of a Devonian may easily be distinguished from that of a Cornishman.

Even within the county, which is very large, accent and pronunciation differ considerably. Natives of Appledore, for example have a most distinctive accent. What then IS accent? It is a subtle combination of pronunciation, tone, and voice production. It has an almost musical quality and can range from a soft burr-like sound to a shrill shriek. One lady, who has unwittingly over the years provided me with much material for this book, has a voice which might well shatter glasses at twenty paces!

While English is not a tonal language, as is Cantonese,

the tone, (or tune?) cannot be ignored, and if accent is accepted as being the equivalent to the tune of a language then most Devonians know the tune but many have forgotten, or have never learned, the words.

Anyone may learn the words, but it is difficult to learn the tune and foreigners, even local foreigners like me, who attempt to speak in dialect by using the words AND the accent can easily cause amusement or can easily give offence, because local people sometimes think that they are being mocked. This is regrettable because not only does one not want to give offence, but it drives true dialect deeper and deeper underground.

We now come to a most important point; Bowring referred to mispronunciation, and fell into what I consider to be the arrogance of claiming that dialectal pronunciation is merely a quaint way of pronouncing standard English. I am certain that this is the wrong approach. Many educated and cultured people use variations of pronunciation which have nothing to do with their regional origins. The simple word *off*, which, to most, rhymes with *toff*, is frequently pronounced as if it were spelled *orf*. Similarly the word *golf* is often pronounced *goff*. Which of these is the correct pronunciation? There is much evidence to suggest that pronunciation changes with the times. In August 1981 a writer in the *Daily Telegraph* commented on the recent phenomenom of the glottal stop in the speech of educated people. It described the Prince of Wales as having a 'classical, rather old-fashioned' accent but accused his Princess of pronouncing the words *quite easy* as *qui' easy*. One must also consider and wonder at the arrival of the long A which is affected by many young persons. Simple words like *black, that, cat* and *rat* appear to have developed an extra long vowel sound, perhaps by a swing of a linguistic pendulum from the old fashioned prissy speech which caused these words to become *bleck, thet, ket* and *ret*?

Reference to eighteenth century poetry indicates that some words may once have been pronounced in a very different way. There are many examples of this. Alexander Pope (1688-1744) used words which in present day English no longer rhyme:

> Good-nature and good sense must ever join;
> To err is human, to forgive, divine.

If Pope really pronounced *join* as *jine,* then this is preserved in Devon dialect. This quotation interested me a great deal and I looked for and found some more. Pope again:

> Whose herds with milk, whose fields with bread,
> Whose flocks supply him with attire,
> Whose trees in summer yield him shade,
> In winter, fire. . .

If *bread* once rhymed with *shade,* then it must have been pronounced as Devonians pronounce it today – *braid.* Again:

> . . .dreading e'en fools, by flatterers besieged,
> And so obliging, that he ne'er obliged. . .

Obliged must have been pronounced *obleeged,* as it still is in Devon. There must be many more examples. Dialectal pronunciation ought not to be dismissed as being a funny way of speaking conventional English. The dialect pronunciation is frequently the original and the present-day standard English word has been derived from it. Dialect is thus frequently a repository of pronunciation and modes of speech once common but now archaic.

There are of course no rules, because dialect has never been and cannot be codified, and pronunciation has always varied from district to district. But some generalised observations can be made:

i. The letter O is frequently pronounced as if it were an A. The word *stop* becomes *stap,* and the word *rot* turns into *rat.*

ii. The double letter O appearing in the middle of a word often sounds like a U. *Stool* becomes *stule, fool* turns into *fule* and *spoon* changes to *spune.*

iii. Paradoxically, words containing the letter U often sound as if they were spelled with a double O. *Bull* becomes *bool,* and *pull* is *pool.* The same sound is heard in some words which have the letters OU or OW in them. *Bow* becomes *boo, mow* changes to *moo* and *plough* is *ploo.*

iv. The sound best spelled ED (as in *head*) is frequently pronounced as if it were spelled AID. *Head* becomes *haid, dead* is *daid, leg* turns into *laig, Fred* into *Fraid* and so on, e.g., '*Fraid staied in baid wi a bad laig, an now er's daid'.*

v. The combined letters AR produce a sound like OR. *Car* becomes *cor, park* becomes *pork* and, of course a *car-park* is a *cor-pork.* (It is interesting to note that this pronunciation survives in many parts of twentieth century USA). A *garden* is often a *gorden,* a *market* a *morket,* one does not play *darts,* but *dorts* and when it gets *dark* it is *dork.* '*Doan't ee work in the pork arter dork!'*

vi. The letter I frequently is pronounced as if it were a double E. *Hill* is *heel, will* is *weel, ill* is *eel.* '*Fraid lived up Torridge eel, but now er's daid and er left no weel'.*

vii. Several words which end with the letters OL, EL, or LE (and therefore in standard English with the sounds EL or OL), are pronounced as if they ended with the letter O. *Mackerel* is *macrow* probably from the French *maquereau,* but *Bristol* becomes *Bristow* because the Old English name of the town was *Bryggstow,* meaning the place of the bridge, and has nothing to do with French. Another word is *trendle* which is pronounced *trendow* (a salting trough), but so far as I am aware, there is no French connection here either. Perhaps it is just easier to say O than it is to say OL or EL.

viii. There is always a tendency to place stress on word endings. Words which in standard English end with the letters ITE but are normally pronounced as if they ended with the letters IT are pronounced as they are spelled. *Favourite* is pronounced *fave-rite,* and *opposite* becomes *oppo-site.*

ix. Initial letters are frequently pronounced in an unusual way. Words beginning with the letters EN sound as if they begin with the letters IN. *Endeavour* becomes *indever* and *enterprising, interprising.*

x. *Every* becomes *ivery.*

xi. The initial letter F frequently becomes a V. *Field* becomes *vield, farmer* is *varmer* and *fen* becomes *venn.* (It is this transposition of initial letters which makes the tracking-down of dialect words so difficult. One can spend hours looking for a word which sounds as if it should begin with a V only to find it, hidden away in the dictionary, under F. The letter F is not the only example, there are many others).

xii. Some say that all countrymen drop their aitches. This is not true. The letter H is not always aspirated, but it frequently is, quite positively and strongly.

xiii. I have seen it claimed somewhere that *zour* is dialect for the word *sour.* It is true that the initial letter S is often pronounced as if it were a Z, but this does not make it a dialect word.

xiv. The initial letters TH quite often sound as if they were DR. This is a very positive transformation and to many people *three* becomes *dree, throat* is *droat* and *thrash* is *drash.*

xv. Other initial letters which are pronounced in an

unorthodox way are UN and words like *uncomfortable,* *understand* and *unlikely* sound like *oncomfortable, onderstand* and *onlikely.*

xvi. There is often a tendency to split vowels and the word *dear* becomes *de-ar, fire* turns into *vi-yer* and *queer* is pronounced as *quee-yur.* Even a simple word like *here,* (usually pronounced *yur*) can become *hee-yar.*

xvii. Words like *really* and *lovely* are frequently pronounced as if they ended with ay. Thus *really* becomes *re-lay* and *lovely* sounds like *love-lay.*

xviii. Letters within words are sometimes transposed, and this process, known as metathesis, turns a familiar standard word into what could be regarded as a dialect word since it is not simply subjected to change by pronunciation, but also by formation. *Crisp* becomes *crips, claps* replaces *clasp, lips* turn into *lisp, urch* is said instead of *rich* and *red* becomes *urd.* There are very many examples including *wapses* or *wapsies* instead of the normal word *wasp.*

xix. The pronunciation of place names is of interest. Many villages and towns are of Saxon or pre-Saxon origin and have the suffix *worthy.* This is the modern spelling of the Saxon word *worthig,* meaning an enclosure, a yard about a house, open place in a village or town or a homestead. Whatever the meaning, the suffix is usually pronounced URY or ERY or ARY, or in at least one case, as REE. *Holsworthy* becomes *Holsery, Bradworthy* is *Braddery, Leeworthy* becomes *Leery* or *Leury, Exmansworthy* becomes *Engsree* and the long place names of *Alfardisworthy* and *Woolfardisworthy* are shortened to *Alsery* and *Woolsery.* In the latter case, even the official spelling has changed and the alternative WOOLSERY is frequently shown on signposts in brackets after the longer WOOLFARDISWORTHY. This is probably done for administrative convenience because the village name is so long. It is most unlikely that anyone has ever given thought to the dialectal reason for the second name. There is a Devon County Council signpost certainly painted by someone with no knowledge that the village name means Wulfheard's Homestead. it proudly points to

WOOLF
ARDISWORTHY

There may be other examples of the grant of official recognition to a dialectal pronunciation, but I do not know of them.

VOCABULARY

THE list of words which follows is of recognisable changes by pronunciation of standard English words. There are, of course many more than I have listed. Some have been deliberately left out because they are of historical interest only and no longer in common use, others have been omitted simply because a line has to be drawn somewhere.

abn haven't
ace yes
aend end
agin against
aich each
aid head
aigs eggs
aikel equal
ail eel
aimzes hames (part of a draught-horses's harness)
ait eat
aither either
aizy easy
all haul
aller alder (tree)

alse (see also **else**) else, otherwise
ango angle
ango-ire angle-iron
angshus anxious
anither another
ankcher handkerchief
ansum handsome
ant am not
apern apron
apmee halfpenny
apn happen
apse hasp (fastening on door) *'Doan't ferget ter apse the gate'*
arbs herbs

arby-pie a pie containing a lot of herbs, parsley, etc.

argify, argy to argue

arken listen, harken

arrant errand

arter after

assards backwards (arse-wards)

ate eat

athout without, unless

attackted attacked

aud old

aughts and crosses noughts and crosses

aut anything

auverdraw overthrow

aveered frightened, afeared

avire on fire

avore before, *'Left and avore'* – left handed

avore-aull after all, for all that

awiz always

awned owned, recognised

awp, awps hope *'Us ken awps ver zunshine'* – 'We can hope for some sunshine'

awt anything *'Do ee knaw awt bout this yer?',* – 'Do you know anything about this?'

awver over

ax to ask, to publish the banns of marriage

axed asked

ayend end

ay-er hair

ay-je hedge

ay-jey-boar hedgehog

ay-jey draw hedge trough, ditch, or drain along the bottom of a hedge

ay-uth earth, soil, the world

ay-ve heave, throw

ayve-mun (aivmin) evening

azides besides

baal bawl, shout, talk roughly

backhouse, backouze back kitchen, wash house

backsivore backside foremost, backwards

baid bed

bain been, bean

baint not going to, *'I baint'* – 'I won't'

bair beer

baistzez beasts (cattle, sheep)

baive beef

bam-bie by-and-by

bard bird

barriole barrel

beeve beef

bellerziz bellows, either for fire, blacksmith, or church organ

bellybon bellyband (part of a horse's harness, a girth)

bequath bequest

be-vower before

biddle beetle

bide stay (abide)

bigotive bigoted

bile boil
bile-in boiling
bimeby later (by-and-by)
bin been
bisky biscuit
bissle beastly, to make dirty
biy boy
bizzens business
blaid bleed
blaiged obliged
blid blood
bloo bloom
blooth bloom, blossom
boddle bottle
bool bull
booty beauty
borry to borrow
bost burst
bouta about
braid bread
brantitus bronchitis
braxis, braxus, brexis breakfast
brimbles, brimmles brambles
brish brush
britiful beautiful
brown titus bronchitis
bule bull
burches breeches
burge bridge
butchin butchering
bye boy

cafender carpenter
cannel candle
casn cannot
cat-ammed (cat-hammed) horses or cattle – or people – who have mis-
shapen legs
caul kale, cabbage
caw-at coat
caze, cause occurrence, case *'Tis usually the cause that dree frostzes be volleyed by rain'*
chack cheek (side of face)
channis challenge, argue with *'I didn't channis er!'*
cheel a (girl) child
chewers chores, tasks
chid chit (allow something, usually potatoes, to sprout before planting)
chimber chamber, an upstairs room
chimley, chimbly chimney
chimley crook the hook in the chimney on which pots or kettles were hung
clat clod (of earth)
claws clothes
climmey climb
cliver clever, well (in health)
cloveray clover hay (hay made from temporary leys as opposed to hay made from permanent pastures)
clurk clerk
con-for-able comfortable
continny continue
coose coarse, rough in the sense of bad workmanship *'I doant like ter zee concrete blocks mixed*

with stones in a dry-stone wall. Looks proper coose, you!'

cornder corner

counton account

cracked correct *'It's cracked to come back'* — 'The correct thing to do is come back'

craim cream

crake creak

crake-along walk with difficulty

crap crop, *crap o teddies* – crop of potatoes

crilly-grains curly greens (type of kale)

crub a crumb, a crust (small piece of bread)

cuz because

Dabn, Debn, Dem, Demshur Devon (Devonshire)

daid dead

dairly dearly

dap tap (hit)

darter daughter

datchin thatching

deave deaf

dee die

deef deaf

deepth depth, something very subtle

dell deal (pinewood or inferior wood)

dezait deceit

dezaive deceive

dirteen thirteen

disnt-naw don't know

dister duster

dithn, dothn does not

doo two, too

doo-bail two-billed mattock

dood done, did *'Er dood it'*

dowel devil

drackly directly (usually means the very opposite – sooner or later)

draive drive

drash thrash

drauved drove (car, horse, etc.)

draw-up throw up (vomit), refer to the past in conversation

drish thrush (bird)

dree three

dray to draw, cart, carry, pull, take. *'Dray a pikchur'* take a photograph

drawed throw

drot throat

drowed throw, thrown

dug dog

dummun old woman

dunnaw don't know

durzant daren't (durst not)

easter eastern

ee, es yes

eel hill

een in

ees fay! Yes in faith! (an exclamation)

Else Alice (name)

empt empty *'It fair empted down!'* – 'It rained very hard!'

erbons ribbons

evelings evenings

feared afraid
feth, fey faith
frit frightened
furnt front

gain going
gaw! cor! (an exclamation)
ge-at gate
ge-at ook gate-hook,
   fastening on gate
genst (hard G) against or
   towards
gee give
ginst, gin (hard G) against,
   towards
gonmer grandfather,
   grandmother
goosegog gooseberry
go'th goes (goeth)
graized greased
grammar grandmother
granfer grandfather
grampy grandfather
grin green
grovel gravel
gurrol girl
gurt great, large
guze goose
gwaine going

hab have
habn have not

hengous heinous, very
   large, terrible,
   tremendous
hey-go! hey-ho!
himperence impudence,
   impertinence
hinderment hindrance,
   delay
hossifer officer
holly holler (shout)
holt hold
huffilant elephant

iggerant ignorant
ijit idiot
infermation inflammation
injin engine
innards inwards (as in
   'inward parts')
intertainment entertainment
iss* yes
izzel himself

jean gin
jidge judge
jolk jolt
jumbo-zale jumble sale

kay key, quay
ketch catch
kit kite, any hawk or bird
   of prey
knacked knocked
koncekense consequence

* This is a less of a word than an indrawn breath between the
teeth and over the tongue. It signifies 'yes', or general agreement,
an indication of sympathy, or merely an invitation to the person to
whom one is listening to carry on with his tale.

krackt correct
kwai-it quiet

lade laden, load
laf lath (as in lath and plaster)
laffed laughed
laig leg
lain lean
laive leave
laanch launch
larn learn
law a load
leaf leave (as in furlough)
leel little
leet little
lem eleven
lent loaned
lew loo, lee (sheltered from the wind)
lewness being sheltered from the wind
lewth a shelter or something that gives protection from the wind
lewzide sheltered side (of hedge or building)
lookee! see! (look thee!)
losting losing
louster litter, waste by littering, (conversely) work hard *'Them as can't scheemy* (scheme or think) *must louster'* – if one is not brainy, one has to work with one's hands
luvver lover (usually term of endearment as opposed to the more usual meaning)

maddick mattock
maister master, boss, Mr
margit market
marvels marbles
mashes marshes
masony masonry, working as a mason
mauth, mose moss
ma-ur moor, wet ground
mazed, maized amazed, daft
me-art might
meel meddle, interfere with
meeze mice
min, mun man, 'them'
mokus monkey
morket market (some parts of North Devon)
moulder mould
mulkee to milk
mushelroom mushroom
mux muck
muxy mucky, muddy or dirty

nair near, mean, tight-fisted
nawed knew
nawse nose
nawtiz notice
neeze sneeze
niver never
noan none
nointed wicked (anointed, used in the sense of the devil's anointed)
nort naught, nothing
norther northern
nother neither, another

nuff enough

ockerd awkward
Offy Alfie, Alfred (name)
omm oven
oncomferable uncomfortable
ondaicent indecent, uncivil
ondaicentness indecency
one-tother one-another
onlight alight (from a car, horse, etc.)
on-nawin unknowing
onpossible impossible
onproper improper
onthaw to thaw (something)
onwriggler irregular, uneven, unpunctual
ood wood
ook hook
oo-mun woman
ope open
ort aught, nothing, ought
orted hurt, injured
ormers alms
orwiz always
owdacious audacious
owzum-iver however

paice peace, piece
palled turned pale
paltrige partridge
pankin panting
passel parcel, quantity, package, collection
passen parson
pauss post
pawer poor, pour, to cram or to stuff full

peel pillow
peel-bears pillowcases
peg pig
pernt print
pimrose, primrose
pisky, piskie pixie
pisky laid caused to lose one's direction by the pixies
pitchin pitching, throwing
pittis pitty
planchin planking, floorboards
plat plot of land
polyanties polyanthus
pool pole, poll, top of head
popple, popplestone pebble, pebblestone
posses, postses posts (usually gate-posts)
powsen poison *'When us fust got mains watter, twas just like powsen! Us cuddn't make a propper cuppa tay'*
prang prong, hayfork
prapper proper, good, satisfactory
primrosen, primrose
pun upon
purtickly particularly
purvekshun perfection

queear queer
quelstring sweltering, very hot (weather)
quot, quat squat, stoop (used about any animal which flattens itself on the ground to escape observation)

raich reach
rail revel, jollification
rames remains, remnants, skeleton
rare raw (underdone)
rasselin wrestling
ratted rotted
raud road
raw row
re-diklus ridiculous
rid red
rile royal
rin run
risty rusty
rittle rattle (in the throat), *rittling* – heavy or hard breathing
rouster rouser, someone making a great noise
rout rut, wheel track
rowcast rough-cast
rummage rubbish

sassy saucy, lively, spirited
sauger soldier
saw soul *'I'm veared to me saw'* – 'I'm frightened to my soul' – frightened to death
scabby shabby (dirty trick)
scat scatter or throw, *go scat* – to go bankrupt. (See *squat)*
scollard scholar
scritch shriek
scruff scurf or dandruff
sex sect (either Church or Chapel)
shape sheep

shaw show (as in County Show)
shet shut, shoot
shillett shale, sedimentary rock
shitten, shitty, paltry, mean, base, contemptible, dirty
shoole shovel
shore-nuff sure enough, certainly, no doubt
showel, shoel shovel
shreed shred
sife, sify sigh
siggle giggle, snigger, titter
sinney sinew
sive scythe
sivver several, a good many
skeen skin
skimmish squeamish
skivver skewer (made of wood)
slome, slone sloe (the fruit), the blackthorn
smarless smallest
solger soldier
souther southern
spake speak of, talk about
speckerty speckled (usually applied to poultry e.g. *'a speckerty hen')*
spuddlin struggling, poking about
spuddle to struggle, kick, resist capture, to be busy in a useless way
spurticles spectacles
squat to squash, crush,

squeeze, *'go squat'* – to go bankrupt. (See *scat*)

staint to staunch, *'staintin blid'* – to staunch a flow of blood

standing a standing place in a market or a stall for horses or cattle

stanks stinks

stann! stand still! (to horse)

stapped stepped

starded started

stauld stolen

stauve stove

steep to stoop

stent stunt, to cause to cease to grow

sterrage a 'stir up' (fuss or commotion)

steve to stiffen, to be stiff, to be numb, to freeze (mostly used of frost or cold)

stiffel stifle

stoopid stupid

stram slam, to bang

stub stump (of a bush or piece of wood)

stugged stuck (in the mud or snow)

stummick stomach or appetite *'A gude stummick to ee wun an all'*

sudger, sodger soldier

tar tear, break, be in a passion or rage

tarnal eternal

taw'd toad, an *'old taw'd'* –

a person, *'poor ol taw'd'*, *'silly ol taw'd'*

tay tea (usually the meal)

tayjess tedious

teddy, tiddy potato

tegeddle tea-kettle

tegeddle-brauth, tiggitle-brauth tea-kettle broth (bread soaked in milk and served with butter, salt and pepper)

tiddivate tittivate

tiddn tis not, it isn't

titch-en-tight touch and go

toze tease, as in disentangling, to comb or card wool

trade tread

traw, trow trough

turmits turnips

turrible terrible

twadden it was not

twick tweak (to jerk suddenly)

ugs puddin hogs pudding (a local kind of pork sausage)

ulse else

ungered hungry

upauver up above (up over)

upzot upset

urch rich

urd red

uthout without, unless, except

vahl fall, a fall of rain or snow

vaityers features (looks)
vall fall (as in America) autumn
vall back, vall edge come what may (heads or tails)
valley value
var far
varder farther
vardist farthest
varmer* farmer
varmering farming
varmint vermin
vast fast, eager
vatches vetches (*leguminosae*)
vaur before, in front of, until
vaur-day before day – before daylight
vaurn for him (for 'un)
vaur-parrut the forward part, front
vaur-um 'Get in front', 'Get before them' – a shepherd's order to his dog to get in front of his sheep
vayacles vehicles
veared afraid (feared)
veesh fish
vencrake fen-crake, landrail, corn-crake
venn fen
ver far
verder further
verdist furthest

vetch fetch
vethervaw feverfew (plant)
vetinry veterinary surgeon
vew few (*'quite a vew'* is a considerable number)
viredug fire-dog, andiron
vittles victuals (food)
vitty fitting, suitable, correct
vittyness fittingness, dexterity, neat-handedness
vlay flee
vlid flood
vlies flies
vloor floor
vlower flower
voaks folks, people, work people
volley to follow
voot foot
vor before, in front of
vore on, forward, going forth, four
vorenoon morning (forenoon)
voretoken forewarning
vot fault
votees photographs
vrim from
vry fry
vule fool
vur, vaur for
vurriner foreigner, any stranger (even from the next village)

---

* Still used as a title. One will greet a person 'Good morning, Farmer', or 'Do you know Farmer Wonnacott?'

vur-why for why? Why,
     because (in a statement)
vuzz furze, gorse

waarn warrant
wad whet (a scythe or
     knife)
waj wedge, bet or wager
walvin wallowing, rolling
     in dust as do fowls and
     animals
ware, wur weather
way with
way-in within
way'n with him
wellzaid well said (an
     indication of approval)
werry weary
wester western
whiles while, whilst ·
whippintree whipple tree
     (draught bar for horses)
why'n ee why don't you
wick weak
wive wife
Wi-yum William
wopsey wasp
worts, urts whortleberries
wude would
wurd hoard
wurdle world
wuth worth
wuts oats

yaffer heifer
yap to bark (yap) like a
     terrier
yappin yapping (talking a
     lot)

yarbs herbs
yaw ewe (a sheep)
yaw cat female cat
yer an ear, here, to hear,
     come here
yerd tell heard (heard tell)
yerzel yourself
yet heat
yettin heating
yeth heath, heather
yurrin a hearing, trial

zackly exactly
zad the letter Z
zaive sieve
zalt salt
zand sand
zap sap (in wood or
     vegetables)
zartain certain
zauney simple, (daft)
zebun seven
zeed-out to seed out, sow
     land with grass seeds
zel self
zex, zax zax (a chopping
     tool used by slaters)
zex sect (Church of
     England, Methodist, etc.)
zhure sure, certain
zie, zieth a scythe
zill sell. *'Nort fer zill'* –
     nothing to sell
zim to seem *'I zim'* – 'it
     seems to me'
zin sun
zinney sinew
zixteen sixteen
zlatter scatter

zoonder sooner (rather)
zore sore
zot sat
zummat something
zupper supper
zwar, zwaur swathe
zye scythe

Chapter 2

GRAMMAR

GRAMMAR is defined by the OED as 'That department of the study of a language which deals with rules . . . the system of inflections and syntactical usages. . .'

Eric Partridge, in *Usage and Abusage,* warned students to beware of falling into the error of supposing that there was such a thing as a universal grammar which was applicable to every language. He stressed that grammar has no existence apart from language. It is, in short, a set of rules codifying usage and it does not pre-determine usage. Grammar is made for man, not man for grammar.

It is certainly clear that what was at one time held to be grammatically acceptable, may readily become unacceptable and *vice versa.* The grammar of dialect must not be dismissed as being wrong simply because it departs from or does not conform to rules which now govern standard English usage.

In 1877 Elworthy published a paper on the grammar of West Somerset, and Pearse Chope, in his paper on the dialect of Hartland, agreed that it was not unlike the grammar of the North Devon dialect. Sarah Hewett went to some lengths to comment on grammatical construction in 1892, but all three were perhaps attempting to codify a language form which cannot be codified without hastening its disappearance. Indeed, it was the declared purpose of the academics of the seventeenth and eighteenth centuries to superimpose grammatical rules upon the rude speech of their times and so to produce a standard language.

Despite this, there are certain patterns of speech and usage which are of interest, so long as it is recognised that they are NOT rules, and never have been. If they were to be made into rules, this would further help destroy that which many seek to preserve.

PLURAL ENDINGS

ELWORTHY claimed that there were eight forms of plural terminations in West Somerset Dialect nouns. I suspect that three of these are now obsolete, but five certainly still exist, and whilst there are countless examples, I list below one of each, showing first the standard English word in its singular form, then the dialect version in the singular and in the plural.

1. rheumatic	roomatik	roomatiks	(ending s)
2. fool	vool	voolz	(ending z)
3. frost	vrost	vrostez	(ending ez)
4. child	cheel	chiller	(ending r)
5. wasp	wapse	wapzies	(ending zies)

SIMILES

Elworthy and Sarah Hewett gave a lot of space to similes and there are enough of these to fill a book. I will list just a few.

Many refer to degrees of stupidity. *Daft as a handcart, mazed as a brish, queer as Dick's hatband.* (Nineteenth century 'as queer as Dick's hatband, that went nine times round and would not meet'.)

A lot of similes refer to degrees of anger or fierceness. *Wild as an awk, wild as a badger, mad as a Scot, mad as a Irish.*

Others of interest are *straight as a gun barrel, whist as a winnard* – meaning as miserable as a heron. (I like this one because nothing looks quite so miserable as a grey heron standing by a stream). Something or someone can be *Zour as a grab* (crab-apple), and one frequently hears the slightly indelicate but graphic expression, as *tight as a fish's* (or *duck's*) *arse.* This is used to describe either a degree of physical tightness, or someone who is tight-fisted. One can be *as poor as a coot,* and in the end a person or a thing can be *daid as a stump.* It would be interesting and amusing to make a complete collection of Devonian similes, and perhaps, one day, I shall – but not yet!

EE AND ER

IN Devon, as in other counties where tourists visit, dialect is not always treated sensibly either by the locals, who ought to know better, or by new-comers who also ought to respect the language of their adopted county, or by visitors who simply come to enjoy themselves. There are many examples of cashing-in on dialect and making fun of it. Souvenirs of all kinds, postcards, china mugs, probably made in Hong Kong, and calendars are inscribed with 'local' sayings designed to bring a smile to the faces of the uncomprehending foreigner. The apparent misuse of the masculine and feminine third person singular pronoun gives rise to much amusement. One of the popular sayings to which I refer is 'In Debn, ee's an er, an' er's an ee, all 'ceptin' my Missus' ol' tom cat, an' even ee's an er!'

The use of the word which *sounds* like ER or UR, is not necessarily a bucolic idiosyncrasy, although in some contexts it is an unaspirated *her*. The OED records that the word *her* is a close relative to the Dutch *Heer* and the German *Herr* both of which are masculine. The word was originally used as a form of address to superiors and is connected with the word *hoary* ('hoary with age', meaning venerable). A *here-man* was a Lord or Master, and the OED gives many examples of the use of the masculine word *here* during the ninth to fourteenth centuries. It says that the word is 'used by Welsh or Gaelic speakers for he, him, or for the speaker himself. . .' and Halliwell (c.1847), records that in the West of England *er* meant *he*. It still does, at least at times.

Whether or not the sound *er* is an unaspirated *her* or a word in its own right, the masculine *er* is undoubtedly used, but so is the masculine *he* and *him* and *his*. These are also frequently used for obviously feminine things. One will hear it said of a cow, for example, *'he's* off his food but *he's* suckling *ee's* calf'.

The second person singular is still quite often *thee,* and this is abbreviated to *ee. Thee* (thou) *art* becomes *thee-rt* or even *thee't.* The words *thou, thine* and *ye* are in daily use but the word that sounds like *ee* can be just an unaspirated *he.* It may however, be an abbreviated *ye,* or *thee. 'Do'st ee?'* means doest thee?

BIST

THE Anglo-Saxon word *bist* is in regular use. It means as it has always meant *art* or *thou art.* Chope gave two examples in 1881: 'Thee bist the biggest vule I ever did zee!' and 'Bist gwain vor to do aught today?' These are as alive today as they were a hundred years ago.

US

THE word *us* is used rather curiously, but regularly, as a nominative: *'Us* be gwain ter morket' or *'Us* be sot be the vire'.

TH

IN the present tense, the ending *th* is used in the third person singular and the first and second persons plural: *It goeth, it rinneth* (runs), *us calleth, they telleth, yer liveth, er putteth,* and as an old lady once said to me about the weather, 'Us must take what *cometh!'*

LIKE

ONE frequently hears expressions such as 'Er sings *loud-like'* (meaning that someone sings loudly), or 'Doctor comed *quick-like*', which is self-explanatory.

The suffix *like* is what remains of the middle English *lich* which has become the standard English suffix *ly*. Thus, what sounds like *loud-like* and *quick-like* might more properly be spelled *loud-lich* and *quick-lich*. *Angered-like* means very angry and 'Er can't hear *much-like*' means that he is very deaf.

THAT, WHAT FOR

THE word *so*, when used to describe a degree of something (so cold, so angry), is often replaced in dialect by the word *that*. 'I were *that* cold' or 'Us wus *that* angered'. The simple question *why?* is often replaced by *what for?* '*What vor* did 'ee do that?'

ELSE

THE dialectal use of the adverb *else* is particularly interesting and serves to indicate the antiquity of the dialect language form. In modern English the adverb invariably follows an indefinite pronoun meaning either *in addition* or *instead*, ('Anything else?' or 'What else?'). This was not always so. In its original use the word had a force of its own and was an adjective used absolutely. It is still so used in dialectal speech: 'Hurry up cheel, us'll be late *else*!' 'Betterway mend that roof, it'll leak *else*!' The OED gives several examples of this original usage and I have found several in Shakespeare. The best, because of its direct relationship with present day Devon dialect, is in King Henry VIII in which the Lord Chamberlain says 'Come, good Sir, we shall be late *else!*'

TO

THE preposition *at* is often replaced by the word *to*. The examples are self-explanatory. 'Where's e *to?*', 'Last

Tuesday us was *to* Bideford', 'Us'll do un *to* dinnertime'.

It is interesting to note that in many cases the word to is replaced by the word for. In archaic standard English the two words were frequently used together e.g: 'She went to market, her eggs *for to* sell', 'But what went ye out *for to* see?', 'Simple Simon went a fishing, *for to* catch a whale'.

In Devon dialect, the word *to* has disappeared leaving only the word for (*fer*). The above quotations would become 'Er went *fer* market, er eggs *fer* zill', 'But what went 'ee out *fer* zee?', '. . . a fishing *fer* catch a whale'.

More common phrases which are used every day: 'I want *fer* knaw' ('I want to know'), 'I've got nort *fer* zill' ('I've nothing to sell'), 'Us went *fer* Bideford' ('We went to Bideford').

The word *to* is also used in the sense of belonging to. 'There baint no key *to* this door'. 'Be there a garden *to* this cottage?'

YOU

MANY statements end with the word *you!* This merely adds emphasis. 'My, tiz cold, *you!*' implies that it is really *very* cold indeed. There are many examples in which the word you becomes a kind of verbal exclamation mark. 'Speaks of rain, *you*' or 'Wot be bout, *you?*'

SINGULAR AND ADJECTIVAL ENDINGS

IT is of more than passing interest to note that, while the plural form of an ancient word is retained in standard English, sometimes the singular occurs only in dialect. Perhaps the best example is the word *brethren* which, though archaic, is still used particularly in place names, such as Seven Brethren. The singular, *brether* is the dialect word for *brother*. In rather the same way some adjectives which are no longer in common use describe nouns which are still with us. *Glassen* is the dialect word for something made of glass, and *cloamen* is something made of cloam (clay). There is no rule and the process is reversed in the modern adjective *iron* which describes the dialect noun *ire*, which means iron. (See *bar ire,* and *ango ire*).

THE grammar of dialect is often mixed with ungrammatical present day English. It is easy to confuse the two and difficult to decide where one ends and the other starts. It could even be that what we now regard as ungrammatical English is, at least in part, a survival of dialectal usage.

Chapter 3

WORDS AND THEIR USAGE

IT is probably the unusual use of standard English words, flavoured with local accent and pronunciation, which most bewilders or amuses visitors to the county.

Ordinary words acquire new meanings. People, places and meal-times have unfamiliar names, and seemingly meaningless 'noises' are often heard in fields and in farmsteads. In this section I list but a few examples.

NAMES FOR PEOPLE

AN interesting practice survives in Devon, somewhat similar to that which exists in Wales, and perhaps elsewhere, whereby it is not unusual for a person to give him or her self an identifying suffix. There are so many people with the same surnames that additional identification is often necessary. It makes a lot of sense, for example, for a Mr Heard to indicate which one he is out of the 150 or more Heards whose names appear in the North and West Devon and North East Cornwall telephone directory. So a farmer will announce himself on the telephone as *Heard to Southcott* or *John to Southcott,* making positive identification possible. Another may call himself *Eric Binnery* indicating that his Christian name is Eric and he farms at Binworthy, or a woman may identify herself as *Dorothy Waytown* meaning that her name is Dorothy and that she lives at Waytown. There is also a tendency to name people by their occupations. *Fred-down-garrige, Elsie-up-shop* and *Alfie-over-pub* are by no means unusual.

FIELD NAMES

FIELD names, like place names, are a special study. Many are of great antiquity but others are still being awarded. Not two miles from my home there are two fields, one called *In-front-of George's* and the other *Behind-Jack's*. Neither George nor Jack live there any more, but the fields will bear their names until they are buried under the concrete and tarmac of progress, probably long after people have forgotten who George and Jack were.

MEALS

A visitor to Devon can easily be confused by the names given to meals. Lunch is a substantial meal eaten at about ten o'clock and consisting of what most people would normally eat for breakfast. It is sometimes called breakfast or *braxis,* but it is more normally lunch.

What many people in other parts of the country calw lunch is known as dinner. Dinner in the evening is usually reserved for meals eaten in an hotel or for annual functions of Associations and Societies. The usual evening meal is called tea or *tay* and this is eaten at about six o'clock after the evening milking is finished. It is another substantial meal consisting of meat and vegetables followed by cakes, cut-rounds, jam, and cream. One will hear a wife say 'Us must get on ome and cook *tay*'.

To the uninformed perhaps this sounds a little odd, but she means only that she must get home in time to prepare the evening meal.

NOISES

THESE are not words but they are frequently heard and deserve a place in this book.

Ho!ho!ho! (sometimes almost ko!ko!ko! with the k implosive)   A noise made when calling cows to come for milking.

Peg!peg!peg!   A call for pigs.

Loo!loo!loo!   A noise made to frighten
                                 birds or rabbits from corn
                                 or grass which is about to
                                 be cut.

THE MISUSE OF WORDS

CERTAIN standard English words are regularly misused
for no apparent reason. Whether the misuse was once a
deliberate attempt to be amusing and has become
habitual, or whether there has always been a genuine
misunderstanding is impossible to say. Whatever the
reason, certain words are regularly misused and, as such,
have become a part of the dialect of the county.

It is important to treat such misuses with caution,
because some have been created by writers attempting to
give an impression of dialect. A. J. Coles who wrote
under the pen name of *Jan Stewer* said in the preface to his
book *Ole Bisket* that he had not written his book with an
eye to the etymologist, but for the amusement of his
readers. Those who have read Jan Stewer's books will
know that some of his dialect words appear to be his own
invention. He calls the accelerator in his car an *acsillyrater*
and says that it is a good name for it because it acts silly.
He calls the carburettor the *carbreaker,* and whilst it is
possible that he heard someone use these words, they
should not be accepted without question as being true
dialect in general use. Indeed, this is borne out by Jan
Stewer himself who in the glossary of one of his books says
of the word *cherrybim* that he had 'actually heard an old
man so describe a charabanc'.

Nevertheless, the accidental or deliberate misuse of
foreign words is the very stuff of which the English
language is made. Consider for example, the etymology of
the word clove. This word comes from the French phrase
clou de girofle which means nail of *girofle* (the flower), and it

refers to the appearance of the seed which looks very much like a nail of the kind that used to be manufactured by the village blacksmith. Either through a misunderstanding, or more likely because of the inability of the English to pronounce the words correctly, the phrase became shortened and the only word used was *clou.* This in turn evolved into clove, so the English cook who puts a clove into a rice pudding or a baked apple is putting a French nail into it. The story does not end there. The second part of the French phrase *(girofle)* still survives but has turned into the word *gillyflower,* the countryman's name for either a wallflower or a species of pink that is known to many as a clove pink, because it smells like a clove.

It is no more, or less, amusing to speak of putting a French nail into a pudding than to use some of the phrases which follow.

'*Arrest* assured I be all right!'

'Er's lookin' up 'er *auntcestors'* (ancestors)

'Er's a bit *bigotive* like!' (bigoted)

'That roof be leakin' like a *calendar'*

'Our Emily is bein' *created* over Barnstaple crematorium'

'Where be they *destructions* for this yer tractor?' (instruction manual)

'They say us've gotter 'ave one of they ole *distinguishers'* (fire extinguishers)

'Be I *illegible* for a grant?'

'If our speaker doant turn up zoon, us'll have ter *impoverish* summat' (improvise)

'Be you *intimidating* that I doant knaw wot I be tellin' about?' (intimating)

'I be aveared of they dirty Atom bombs! One of these days us'll get 'urtled into *maternity*!'

'Our Bert 'ad to see one of they ole *physical therapists'*

'I woant 'ave they childer *protruding*' (intruding)

'If us goes in they woods, us'll get *persecuted*' (prosecuted)

WORDS AND PHRASES

THE selection of words and phrases which follow are used in every day speech, and represent a very important part of the dialect of Devon.

In order to present them in reasonable order I have selected the principal word in each phrase or sentence and used this to determine its alphabetical place in the list.

A

take un abroad take it to pieces

next akin close to, almost *'Er weren't daid, but next akin to it'*

all so well just as well

'I allow that the lifeboat got too near they rocks' *'I believe that'* (this is an example of a word which is no longer in general use in England but which survives in dialect and is used in present-day American speech)

back along a while ago, some time ago, years ago

wild as an awk (hawk) very angry, very fierce (animal or human)

B

go back, going back to deteriorate. *'Er's goin back vast'* – he, or it, is deteriorating rapidly

back ouse (house) back kitchen, scullery, lean-to, wash house

bacon-aid (head) dunce, stupid person

wild as a badger angry

a belly like a Barnstaple man, a bum like a Barnstaple woman pot bellied, anyone, male or female, with a big backside. It may be merely because the letter B looks vaguely like a bulging human figure but it has been suggested to me that the expressions, quite frequently heard, relate to the relative prosperity of Barnstaple in the past, which could perhaps have caused its citizens to grow fat. I consider that it is more likely to be derogatory in intent and related to the long-standing differences between Bideford and Barnstaple, whose citizens still argue and even fight over the number of ships each

port sent to fight the
Spanish Armada in
1588.

**'Where was you to beer,
Sunday?'** *'Which pub did
you patronise last Sunday'*

before superior to, better
than *'Ridin is before
walkin'*

better way one had better,
it is better that one
should (Another example
of a phrase which is lost
in standard English but
survives in modern
American usage

boy chap an unimportant
or unimpressive young
man

bettermost volk Not *gentry-
folk, bettermost* folk are
probably best described
as upper-middle-class
people

between the two lights
twilight (the two lights
being the sun and the
moon)

my Bird a form of
affectionate address
between people, male to
female, female to female
or even male to male

blackaid (black-head)
tadpole

black drish (thrush)
blackbird

black tail a stoat

me booty *'My beauty';* a
form of address to men,
women, and animals
quite indiscriminately,
irrespective of the sex of
the speaker or of the
person or animal being
addressed

bow bend, *'See if you can
bow un straight'.* This is
interesting usage because
in standard English the
word bow tends to imply
the bending into a curve
something that was once
straight. In Devon it
means to bend into a
curve *or* to straighten
something that is bent

brave an amplifying word
'a brave lot' – a lot, *'a
brave ol uproar'* – an
unpleasant state of
confusion or noise. The
word also means well or
fine; *'Ow be gettin on then?*
– 'How do you do?'
(answer) *'Brave, oh brave!'*

break to tear. One *breaks* a
piece of cloth

bullocks any bovine
animal, including dairy
cattle. Dairy cows are
milking bullocks

C

canvas linoleum, floor
covering including
modern equivalents of
linoleum

caper any activity or

happening. A general
election might be called
'Thees ol lection caper'.
There is often a
suggestion of disapproval
of the subject under
discussion

cheel (child) a baby girl.
Parents of a new-born
baby will be asked *'Be it a
biye or a cheel?'* The word
is also used as a term of
endearment between
husband and wife

chilled slightly warmed,
(taken the chill off) *'Us've
chilled the watter'*

clever in good health.
Normally used in a
negative sense; *'Er baint
too clever, you!'* This
means that the person
concerned is very unwell

coller en aimzes collar and
tie. The collar and
hames are part of a
working horse's harness
and go around the
animal's neck; *'Us puts on
coller en aimzes ter go ter
chapel'*

coller work very hard
work. The expression
dates from the time when
a working horse pulling a
heavy load pressed hard
into its collar

couple a ewe with lambs.
A single couple is a ewe
with one lamb, a double
couple is one with twin
lambs and a sheep with
triplets is a triple couple

passel of ol crams
something not worthy of
credence

criterion consideration,
importance. Usually used
negatively *'That baint no
criterion'*

cross way a road junction.
A four cross way is a
normal cross road. A
three cross way is a T or
Y junction

D

my dear not usually a term
of affection although it is,
of course, used in the
normal context. It is
more likely to be used as
a form of address to
anyone, not necessarily
known to one.

demand command; *'Stay
there an you'll be able to
demand both ways'*, said to
sentry or watchman or
any person appointed to
be a look-out for any
purpose

**dirty shame, dirty
furriner** a word of
amplification normally
implying something
tiresome or troublesome.
A dirty shame means a
terrible shame and a

dirty foreigner means someone from a long way off (as opposed to an ordinary foreigner who could be just someone from the next parish) *'I've not done a dirty thing in my garden'* means that little has been achieved in the garden. The word dirty is only used to mean unclean when standard English is being mixed with dialect. The dialect word for dirty is *bissle*

distinct distinguish, see clearly, recognise *'I couldn't distinct un proper'*

dough baked half baked, silly, soft in the head

Er drashed un wi watter drenched

dry-belly a miser

E

goodnight each goodnight everybody

F

proper fashion used to amplify a statement, it means 'well and truly' *'Us be znawed-een proper fashion'* **put fast** fasten, close, shut (door or gate)

fetch the pump prime the pump to produce sufficient suction to allow it to raise water

firelights kindling wood for lighting fires (as opposed to *sticks* which are logs)

my flower another normal form of address between friends of either sex. I have heard this used as a form of address between two robust and very masculine farmers

forestry a plantation managed by the Forestry Commission. *'Our Trevor works up forestry'.* One also goes for a walk *'in the forestry'*

frightened surprised *'I were frightened to zee zo many volk up Church'*

G

gentry volk gentry, upper-class people

serve ee glad it serves you right

that do make the gravy run hard work that makes one sweat

bout a gunshot a measure of distance (said to be approximately the distance between two telegraph poles)

H

only half a load simple, not quite right in the head

play Hamlet kick up a fuss, create a scene. *'Er didn't alf play Amlet!'*

daft as a handcart stupid, silly

hansome beautiful, worthy of praise, good. *'A hansome morning'*, or *'Ow be then my flower?'* (answer) *'Ansome me dear, proper ansome'*

me handsome yet another normal form of address, friendly but not necessarily familiar

Us'll zee wot the weather happens 'We will see what happens to the weather'

a proper harem-scarum tow'd a rascal, a wild uncontrolled person

queer as Dick's hatband strange, unusual, odd person

up th'eel (hill) on higher ground, particularly on the moors. *'Er varms up th'eel'* probably means that he farms on Exmoor or Dartmoor

a hinderment a delay *'Us met wi a hinderment'*

Us can't call him home 'We cannot remember him'

The watter was up home to the tap o'me butes 'The water came up to the top of my boots'

hundreds a lot, plenty, many; *'Come on een, there's undreds of room'*, or *'Us've got hundreds of grass you!'*

(Until about 1469, the word *hundred* merely meant more than five score)

I

ignorant (iggerant) bad mannered, badly brought up, foolish or uncouth behaviour. *'Doan't ee take no notice of Bill Brewer, er's propper iggerant'*, said of a rude, outspoken Parish Councillor

J

job a happening, an event (see *caper*) *'Thees ol lection job'*

K

kidneybean (bain) runner bean

L

learn (larn) teach

a litany of complaints a long list of complaints

long-sleeve clock a grandfather clock

long-sleeve hat a top hat

long-tailed rabbut a pheasant (sometimes shot without a game licence, when it is 'mistaken' for a rabbit)

M

made meanings to make facial signs or gestures

maid a little girl, a young woman not necessarily a virgin, a term of endearment used by a man addressing his wife no matter how old she might be

manys-a-time often

marvellous something at which to marvel. In modern speech the word usually means something good. Not in dialect. *'Tiz marvellous ter zee zuch bad ploughin'*

master another amplifying word; *master big* – very big, *master small* – very small *master cold* – very cold. (The word is pronounced very much as in standard English, but mister (Mr) a word derived from master, is pronounced *maister*, retaining the old French pronunciation *maistre*)

manful powerful *'Baint manful enough you!'*

mazed as a brish daft, stupid, (a *brish* is a brush, although why a brush should be stupid I do not know)

by his mind of his own free-will *'Er wouldn't go up Doctor's by ee's mind, but us made un'*

no mistake still another amplifying phrase *'Us be znawed een, no mistake!'*

mortal, mort a considerable quantity, very. Used to amplify *'There's a mortal lot ov it about', 'I'm a mortal onlucky ol chap', 'There wus a mort of volk up Church'*

N

near mean, tight-fisted

about nort doing nothing, idle *'Av'ee got a lorry about nort?'* 'Have you got a spare lorry?'

zhure nuff (enough) yet another phrase of amplification *'Us be znawed een, zhure nuff!'*

O

ordained ruled, agreed, decided *'T'was ordained fur me to do the job'* a phrase often used instead of 'yes please'

don't make a bit ov odds I don't mind if I do

P

passel of rummage (rubbish) a parcel of rubbish, nonsense

parish lantern the moon

pick in bring in (one picks in the washing from the clothes line)

us keeps pickin (picking) 'We keep on going', 'We carry on somehow'

Er laffed like a piskie he laughed maliciously (like a pixy)

pity hole grave

tiz like workin wi a

busted prangstick
literally, 'Like working with a hayfork with a broken handle' – working under great difficulty with everything against one

proper good, excellent, 'That will do nicely', 'thank you', 'Proper job'

where did ee go to pub? 'which pub did you go to?'

they aven't punished ee too much then! 'You look very well despite what they [the doctors] have done' (said to me after a major operation)

R

er's a propper riptackle 'She [a little girl] is a real tomboy'. The word dates from the days of horse-drawn implements when a badly broken horse would rip the harness (tackle) to pieces

S

Give him fair scope give someone the benefit of the doubt (perhaps unwisely), giving someone too much room for manoeuvre in questionable circumstances

mad (or **wild**) **as a scot** very angry, fierce

several really rather a lot *'There was several volk up Churchyard'*

sidling ground steep ground, difficult to cultivate

spaiks (speaks) of rain 'It looks like rain.' In modern times it may be the Radio or TV weatherman, but in earlier days one would hear *'Spaiks ov rain you, leaves be turnin' up'*

stag a cock-bird amongst hens

sticks logs, tree trunks. See *firelights*

swettin straims perspiring very freely

T

teddy fat weather damp warm weather which makes potatoes grow fat

telephone English speaking consciously without use of accent, idiom, or dialect. Many country people virtually speak two languages, their natural dialect amongst themselves and a language reserved for communicating with foreigners (on the telephone)

telling speaking *'Wot be telling bout?'*

terrify, terrification

teasing *'I do like to terrify they boys'*

thunder and lightning bread spread with golden syrup and cream

ticket bill, invoice, any important bit of paper

times often, frequently *'I've telled ee times'*

toad person, usually with overtones of pity or dislike *'Poor ol toad', 'zum careless toad', 'zilly ol toad'*

tongue pie a nagging, scolding

travel to move across the ground *'Tis too wetty ter travel'*

travelling visiting (surreptitiously) *'Er's travellin niddimes',* said of a married woman believed to be visiting a lover

two-to-once dealing with more than one matter at a time

U

er's gone up shop one generally goes *'up shop'* or *'up Church'* or *'up our Emily's'*

upright twelve midday (or midnight) exactly on the hour (upright four, five, six, etc.)

keep upsides with keep up with, be as good as

V

valiant agressive

viddle fiddle (violin), an instrument for sowing grass seed

'Gid vore roun, dug!' an order given to a cattle or sheep dog to get round in front of the flock or herd

W

every whip and trip, every whips while every now and again

Whitsunday stitchwort (flower)

wicked angry *'I feel propper wicked!'*

workish weather usually in negative form *'Baint workish weather, you!'* Too hot, or too pleasant to go to work

made wise pretended, put on an act

Z

baint zackly not exactly right (in the head)

zeem-zo seems to be the case *'They'm zellin varm, zeem-zo'*

Chapter 4

TRUE DIALECT WORDS

IN 1839 *A Devonshire Dialogue in Four Parts* was published. This little book contains a glossary prepared by the Reverend John Phillips which sets out to explain the meaning of the dialect words used in the book. It is a record of conversations between a servant maid called Betty and her lover Robin. It is a simple and pleasant story, refreshing in its innocence, but the most interesting thing about it is not the story or what is contained in the glossary, but what words have been left out.

Whereas many of the words used in the text are carefully explained, even more words, which would now certainly be regarded as dialect are ignored by the editor and are not explained at all. This could be due to inefficient editing, but it is much more likely that such words were in common use in the eighteenth century and were not then regarded as being dialect. This led me to wonder how many of our Devon dialect words I could find in the OED. The search took a long time, principally because of the difficulty of knowing how the word might be spelled. It is frequently impossible to determine with any accuracy even the initial letter of the word or to know, for example, whether the word was originally spelled with a V or an F.

Nevertheless I have succeeded in finding quite a lot of words, although many are said to be obsolete. When I have found a word in its original form, or an obviously related root word, I have shown in brackets the approximate date of its first appearance in writing. This of course in no way fixes the antiquity of the word itself, and one can be certain that it was spoken for many years before it was first written.

Some of the words which I have listed are obsolescent if

not yet obsolete, others are rarely used and are probably known only to a few dialect speakers, but I have included them because, in my experience, having seen a word in an old publication, one quite frequently then hears it used in conversation and *vice versa*. An example of this occurred in the early 1970s. One of our neighbours was an old lady who spent the winter huddled over the fire in her front parlour, seldom appearing in public between October and May. I was therefore surprised one bitterly cold January afternoon to see her at her front door. When I asked what she was doing out on such a beastly day, she replied *'Tiz gwain ter blunk'*, and pointed to the leaden sky. Clearly she meant that it was going to snow, but I had never before heard the word. I asked many local people if they had, but the answer was always the same. I could find nobody who had! I gave up, and thought that I had misheard her, until I eventually found the word in Mr Phillips' glossary. It seems that one can have a *blunk ov znaw* or a *blunk ov vire*, a snowflake or a speck of burnt material, which looks something like a snowflake, rising from a fire. Since I found the word, and the related word *blunkin* in writing, I have heard it several times in casual conversation.

In this section I deal only with definitions and historical origins and not with etymology. This is because whilst in my opinion a word can only be enjoyed to the full if one knows its etymology, sometimes a translation is all that is immediately required by the reader. The etymology of dialect words is covered in the final sections of this book.

VOCABULARY

abew (aboue, c.1596) above
addle-gutter (adelan, c.1000) stagnant gutter or pool

adrowed (adruwode, c.1000) dried
agenst to meet *'Go agenst Feyther'*

aggets (agats – precious striped stones, c.1570) marbles

ail (c.1000) awn (beard) of barley

ailer, hailer (heale – a secret place, c.897, hale – a tent c.1330) tarpaulin, rick cover, horse blanket, someone who conceals a crime or misdemeanour – *'The ailer's so bad as the stailer'* – the person who conceals a theft is as bad as the person who steals

ale-up (halen – to pull up, c.992) to pull up earth around growing plants, particulary potatoes *'us'll ale-up they teddies'*

allen summer good, fine summer

allow (c.1548) to come to a conclusion *'I allow you'm right'*

aneest (anend, c.1325) close to, nearby, nigh

angledog, angletitch (angeltwaeccean, c.940) common earthworm

appledrain, appledrone (OED, but no date given) wasp

aps abcess

arrants article carried when running an errand (not the errand itself)

arrish (edisc, c.700) stubble, what is left in the field after corn has been cut and carried, the after-math of a crop

arrish mooey, arrish-mow (see **mow** and **mooey**) small temporary ricks made of stooks of corn stacked on top of each other to allow rain to drain off when the weather is wet and the corn not yet fit to carry – see also *gook*

auncy anticipate bad tidings, be apprehensive

axen (aescean, c.1000) ashes

axwaddle to wallow on the ground

axwaddler originally a lowly person who went around farms buying ashes to sell to soap makers, now a term of disdain or reproach

bap (bappis, c.1513) small loaves of bread. This word is not confined to Devonshire. See *cut-rounds*

bar-ire (see ire) crow-bar

barleyzears awns of barley

bay-spittle honey

beastings (beost, c.1000) colostrum, the first milk from a newly-calved cow

beaufet (OED, no date) a glass-fronted display cupboard

begayed bewitched

belve (Belwe, c.1305) to bellow or shout, sing loudly *'I do like a hymn wot I can belve out!'*

ben (ben – the inner part, 14th cent.) the truth of the matter, the inside story

biddle to enlarge, to grow bigger *'They onions be biddled'*

billers (billure, c.1440) hollow stems of umbelliferous plants such as cow parsley

billery to be hollow, like a biller

bird, burd (burde, c.1300) a form of endearment, form of address between persons of either sex *'Mornin my burd!'*

bissle to make dirty, to be dirty. Said to a grubby little four-year-old *'Mr Downes doan't like bissle lill maids like you'*

bist (c.1000) are (you), or (you) are *'Bist gwain up shop?' 'Thou bist a prapper vule!'*

biver (beofian – to tremble c.888) to shake, tremble, with cold or fright

bizzy-milk colostrum

blackaid tadpole

blackdrish blackbird

blacktail stoat

bladders blisters

blake (blakien, c.1579) to turn pale, *'Er blaked away'* – he fainted

blake wi laffin to laugh until one cries

blinemares nonsense

bline-mop blindfold

bloath pecker tom tit

blooth, bloath (blooth, c.1602) bloom, blossom

blunkin snowing

blunk ov vire spark or fleck of burnt material

blunk ov znaw snowflake

bodley (Mr George Bodley of Exeter invented a patent cooking stove in 1802) any cooking stove irrespective of its make

bowerly handsome, large

brinded fierce (usually animal)

brist fine dust

brit bruised

brither (c.1300) brother

brithernlaw brother-in-law

buddled suffocated

buldery, buldering sultry weather

butt (c.1796) two-wheeled cart, the body of which is capable of being tipped, used for carrying dung, mangolds, potatoes, often called a *dung-butt;* bee hive. I have seen it in old books used to mean *suddenly,* but I have never heard it used in this context

caal think *'What do ee call you'm doing?'*

canker berry (cankers, c.1582) berry of the dog-rose (hips)

canker-row wild rose, dog-rose

cannel teening candle light

care (c.1849) mountain ash tree

cater cousins (c.1547) intimate friends

cauch mixture, nasty mess

chad, chag gorse

chattermag person given to gossip *'Er's a propper ol chattermag!'*

chauk jackdaw

chibbles (chibboles, c.1362) spring onions, immature shallots eaten raw in place of spring onions, or in a *'chibble pasty'*

chinkin grass the first flush of spring grass

chitterlings (cheterlingis, c.1280) pigs' intestines cooked for human consumption, human intestines *'I b'aint zackly right in me chitterlings, Doctor!'*

chonchables icicles

chuggypig woodlouse (North Devon), a

collection of small pigs (in the plural), the smallest pig in the litter (South Devon). See also *zowpeg* and *nissledraft*

chur hurry, speed

chyney (cheney, c.1634) things made of china

cladgy (cledgie – sticky, cladgy, c.1577) of a waxy consistency (one has *cladgy* varieties of potatoes)

clag, cleg (cleg, c.1449) horsefly

claps (c.1450) clasp on clothing, door, harness *'Please to ondo this yer claps'*

clauvell (clavel, c.1602) beam of wood over a fire-place

clegged, clagged (claggye, c.1570) used to describe the condition of an animal whose hair or wool is covered with dried dung

cloam (clame, c.1000) clay used for making something

cloamen something made of clay

close (clos. c.1489) enclosure (a word frequently used in field names) East *close,* South *close,* Church *close*

clump thump, hit *'Gi un a clump roun the yur-ole!'*

cob (c.1602) building material consisting of mud, clay, straw, bracken, sometimes horsehair, and small stones

coin (coynston, c.1350) corner of building or wall, corner stone

condiddled (c.1746) wasted, spent unwisely

confloption muddle, mixture *'That there's a master confloption, no mistake'*, *'Tis an ol confloption me Missus makes fer me dinner'*

confuddled confused

coose iron tips on toes of hobnail boots *'Take they boots to the cobbler fer coosin an heelin'*

copperfinch cock chaffinch

courtledge (curtillag, c.1206) farmyard

cowflop foxglove

crackety, cracky-wran wren

crams (crams – to fill with false information, c.1794) statements that lack credibility, lies (see *A Parcel of ol Crams* by Jan Stewer)

crazed (crased – to break down in health, c.1476) painful, sore, hoarse, aching *'I be crazed all auver Doctor!'*

creem (c.1746) to squeeze

croosle gossip, to talk confidentially with malice *'They ol women was croosling together'*

crumpetty crooked, awkward, uncomfortable *'This yer arthur-itis do make me lie abed all crumpetty-like'*

cubbert (c.1663) cupboard

culver (culfran, c.825) pigeon, dove

curious (curious – full of care, careful, c.1386) careful *'I were uncommon curious about that job'*

cut-round soft bread roll, usually associated with cream teas (see also *bap*)

dabby nervous disposition *'Er's dabby in the aid'*

dane red-haired man

daps plimsols, cheap canvas shoes

dashel thistle, milky-dashels – sow thistles

datty (see doany) hay which is too damp to carry

daver (rhymes with waver c.1621) to wither

davery-topped plants or flowers that have wilted *'They lettuces be all davery topped. B'aint vit fer ait!'*

dawkawk, dawbake stupid person *'You'm a gurt dawkawk!'*

deeve (deaf c.897) corn with shed grain, deaf

dew snail (dewe snayle, c.1548) large black slug

diddyman small or insignificant person

dimity, dimmit, dimps, dimpsie (dimmit c.1746) twilight, dusk, evening time

discloose bad language

doaney (see datty) something (usually grass or hay) that is damp with the morning dew

doilish (doiled, doilt, doillit, c.1513) silly, fyolish, particularly applied to elderly people *'Poor old toad, er's gettin doilish!'*

dowell (deuel, c.1290) the devil

drade, trade (c.1697) material, substance, almost anything tangible, often used in derogatory sense *'I doant think much to this yer drade'* (workman speaking of a cheap pot of paint) *'Us be gwain ter ave zum of this yer vallin drade'* (it is going to snow)

drags (draggis, c.1388) spike harrows (farm implement)

drangway (drang, c.1787) narrow lane, a passageway

dray (dreihen, c.1225) pull, draw, carry in cart or trailer, *'Us be drayin dung'*, or *'Varmer be drayin stones'*. Also used in reference to photography; *'Drayin a photo'* – taking a photo

drecksill, dreckstool doorstep, threshold

drishel thrush (bird)

drumbledrane (c.1746) bumblebee

dry stone ditch (ditch – raised bank, c.1568) dry stone wall (a wall made of stones without the use of cement) a field bank faced with stone

dryth (drythe, c.1533) degree of dryness *'There's no dryth in it'* – the air is damp

durn (c.1325) a door frame

durn-aid (head) the cross piece at top of door frame, architrave

durndel as above, but usually applied to trim around the door frame

dwindle someone with shoulders hunched with the cold *'I be rumped up like a dwindle!'* (A *dwindle* is something that has shrunk in size or dwindled away)

eaver (c.1732) perennial rye-grass (*Lolium perenne;* a local strain is known as *Devon Eaver*), the flowering heads of any species of grass, a grass field gone to seed and no longer fit to cut for hay or silage *'That vield be all eavered you, baint vit fer nort!'*

eggleberry berry of hawthorn tree

er him, he, it

evil (evall, c.1642) fork

fancical (c.1671) tasteful, critical, particular as to the way work is done

ferry, fairy, vairy, vaire (veir, c.1300) weasel

fitch (c.1550 – a polecat) ferret

flair (flare, c.1847) layer of fat in a side of bacon

flibberts small pieces, smithereens *'Jist then, the ole mare, er rinned agin a wackin gurt big stone, er kicked the trap ter flibberts, an er tratted off alone.'* (Tavistock Goosey Fair. Song written by C. John Trythall)

flicket tantrum, show of temper

flitterings, flittereens small pieces (see *flibberts*)

floppy dock foxglove

flummoxed puzzled, defeated

forestain maintain

fraped (frapped, c.1548) tied up, bound up tightly, cut back (of an overgrown hedge) *'Us'll frape un off, you!'*

frawzey celebration, party, treat *'Us'll have a propper frawzey, ter zelebrate'*

french nuts walnuts

fuzzchat stonechat

galley (gally, c.1660) frighten, alarm *'Did er galley you Missus?'*

gambers (gamba, c.1607) human ankles, hocks of an animal, the joint in the hind leg of a quadruped between the true knee and the fetlock

gee (the G is hard, as in give) give

genst (hard G) by the time something was finished *'Genst er vinished talkin'*

geddout! expression of surprise or incredulity, get out!, really!, not likely! *'Geddout, you'm pullin me laig!'*

NOTE: Almost any word beginning with F can be pronounced as if it began with V

glassen object made of glass

glinney guinea fowl

glint peep, look shyly *'Come on een! Doan ee stan there glintin roun the cornder!'*

glousing glowering

goil (goyle, c.1617) a ditch or gulley

golden gladdi, gladdy (c.1859) yellowhammer

goocoos bluebells

gook small temporary rick built on stubble during bad weather (see *arrish mowey*)

grab (grabbe, c.1578) crab apple

granfer grig a long-legged water insect

granfer longlaigs crane fly, daddy longlegs

greybird thrush (bird)

gridley granular in texture, gritty

grockle visitor, holidaymaker (this unpleasing word, of unknown origin, is believed to be a relative newcomer. It is widely used in North Devon, is normally derogatory and equates to *emmet* (ant), which is what Cornishmen call unwelcome holiday visitors

grubbish hungry

gulch (gulcheo, c.1225) to

gulp greedily, to swallow

gutsing greedy

gyte trick, habit

haler (see ailer) tarpaulin, rick cover, horse blanket

have (rhymes with shave) (havoir, c.1400) behave, usually in the negative *'This yer thing baint bein have'*

harnzee heron

havage (c.1846) ancestry, family background *'Er commeth of good havage'*

heft (c.1558) weigh, weight *'I heft un in me and, twere bout pound en arf'*

heller wild person, naughty child *'Our Will's a proper little heller!'* – the speaker may be rather proud of the child, and that he is a 'chip off the old block'.
  'Er's a proper heller, you!' – the person spoken of is disreputable. *'Tis a proper heller, you!'* – used in conversation about bad weather, politics, a break-down of machinery, or any other misfortune

hicketty a wooden latch on one side of a door, operated by lifting it out of, or lowering it into its wooden 'catch'. If one is on the opposite side of the door one has to put one's finger through a hole bored in the door to lift the *hicketty*

hickymal titmouse

hogs (c.1340) yearling sheep

homescreech misslethrush

hoop bullfinch

hornywink lapwing, at Hartland, North Devon known as a *Braddery* (Bradworthy) *hornywink* and at Coombe Martin as a *Challacombe Hornywink*

horse-long-cripple dragonfly

hyvers (rhymes with divers) an exclamation *'My hyvers!'*, alternative to 'My dear soul!' or 'Bless me!' Literal meaning obscure

ile (ezle, c.1000) a beard or awn of barley

ire (15th cent.) iron (see *bar ire*)

item thing, subject under discussion, *'Wot stupid item be on upon now then?'*

jabber the lower lip of a fish

jonnick true, truly, something is unreasonable, untrue, or unacceptable *'T'isnt jonnick you, t'isnt jonnick!'*

kaky sticky

kickshaw (17th cent.) amusement, exhibition, entertainment

kracketty wren (bird)

lacer, laceing huge *'Tiz a gurt lacer!' 'Tiz a laceing gurt thing'*

lade (c.1502 – load, c.1686 – fixture on cart) load, loaded, full, a ladder-like attachment to cart or trailer designed to increase carrying capacity

larn (c.1300) teach

leary (leer, c.1250) empty, unladen, hungry. If one ploughs a field one way, one is *leary* on the return journey

leat (c.1590) artificial waterway, brook

leer (c.1386) flank (of man or beast)

lend-ay (hay) hay made from permanent meadow grass as opposed to hay made from temporary leys

lent rosens, lent lillies wild daffodils (*Narcissus pseudonarcissus* L.)

lern (c.1300) teach

lickker something remarkable, either good or bad *'Twas a propper lickker!'*

linney (linny, c.1695) lean-to shed. In the old days

one always had a 'cart linney', a covered lean-to in which carts were stored when not in use

long-tailed-pie long-tailed-tit

louster (a word of many meanings) hard work, graft, *'Them as cain't scheemy must louster'* – (people who cannot use their brains [scheme] must work with their hands), to make a mess, to spread litter around, to walk with a swagger

main (c.1632) very much, considerable, powerful

maister (c.1300) Mister (Mr), also normal form of address *'Mornin, Maister', 'Where's Maister to?'*

make-vor fore-shadow, prophesy *'The wind maketh vor rain!'*

make wise pretend, pretence, a sham

mascall caterpillar of the Cabbage White butterfly

master (pronounced marster) a word of amplification *'They be master small bullocks', 'That be a master great marrow'*

maun, maund (maunde, c.1535, mand, c.1725) large round wicker basket with handles attached to rim

maunchuss (maun, c.1774) huge, great *'A maunchuss gurt bullock'*

mauth moss

mawses, mores (moran, c.1000) roots of plants or tree

min (OED, no date) them

mind (mynde, c.1377) remember *'I mind well the time that barn was built'*

mizmaze confusion

mole heave mole hill

mommet (mamet, c.1494) scarecrow, an expression of disdain about a person *'Giddout, you'm a gurt mommet'*

moor (more, c.1441) unproductive farm land, land which has reverted to waste, common land (as in Dartmoor and Exmoor)

moowey, mow, mowhay (muha – a rick, c.725) rickyard (see *arrish mooey*)

mort (c.1694) a lot *'There's a mort o volk up Church, and more down pub'*

mortal (c.1716) very *'It's mortal cold', 'I'm a mortal onlucky ol chap, You've niver yerd zich a caze, From mornin till niuht, Nort never goeth right, Tiz enough to draive any man mazed'* (Trad.)

moundery mildewed

mump-aid (head) stupid person

mun them *'I knawed mun well enough'*

mux muck

mux adrowed dried muck, dust (see *adrowed*)

nackin vore getting along, *'Ow be aul ov ee nackin vore then?'*

nammett (nummet, c.1847) mid morning light meal, snack

natlings intestines

niddick (nuddock, c.1558) nape of neck

nimpingang whitlow, festering spot on finger

nisseldraft smallest pig in litter, a runt (see *chuggypig*)

nittles, nittals hazel bushes

nointed nointed *'He'm deul's nointed'* (Devil's annointed)

obble-de-oy (hobble-de-hoy, c.1540) term of distain *'Zum obble-de-oy gurol wrote this yer letter!'* (said of a letter from a solicitor's office)

onhale uncover (see *ailer* and *ale-up*)

onwray undress

oodwall the great woodpecker

orts (ortus, c.1440) remains of food, remnants, refuse

owdry cloudy

paike tardy person *'Er's a proper ol paike'*. Said of people always behindhand *'They'm prapper paikey, niver gets to morket on time'*

paiken to doddle *'There they wus, paiken along'*

pair o prangs a single dung fork (with four prongs) (see *prang*)

paunched, poached (poching, c.1600) land made muddy and pitted through over-stocking, ground churned up by feet of animals

paunchin removing entrails of rabbits

peendy musty (in taste or smell)

pegslooze pig sty

pick (OED – throw or pitch) pitch fork with two prongs (see *prang*)

pillem, pillum dust

pimplevoot club foot

pinchfart miserly, niggardly person

pinking ailing, weakly, querulous

pinswill (pinswels, c.1591) small abcess or boil

ploo (plew, c.1535) plough

ploo-gide (hard G) ropes used as reins on working horses pulling ploughs or other farm implements

pluff unwell

pook (c.1718) haycock

popples, popplestones (papolstanas, c.1000) pebbles

power (c.1660) great number *'You'll zee a power ov volks down to Exeter fer Debn County Shaw'*

powl to race

powler one who races. (There is a length of road near Woolfardisworthy in North Devon called Powler's Piece. This is the last straight stretch before Cann's Water, whence the road winds all the way to the village. It was here that horsemen, or *carriage volk* used to race to try to get ahead of the carts going to and from the lime kilns at Bucks Mills)

prang (prange, c.1502) hay fork with two prongs

prize (c.1681) fulcrum *'Us caint find no prize fer the bar-ire'* (a person using a crow bar as a lever to lift something cannot find a fulcrum for it)

pucker (c.1741) fuss, commotion

pug (c.1865) sea trout

purt sulking, pouting *'Er's purt an won't say nort'*

pusky short of breath

quarrel (c.1447) pane of glass in a window

quoin (c.1532) corner of building or wall, (see *coin*)

rabbin urdick robin red-breast

raunch vegetable or salad eaten without first being cooked

raymes (rame, c.1497) skeleton, remains of something *'Er only left the raymes of that there pie!'*

revel (c.1350) annual feast day, merry-making

rigmarole (c.1736) much talk or fuss, something too complex to be understood clearly

rory-tory tawdry, loud in colour (usually applied to someone else's dress)

rowdugs (row rhyming with cow) rough, uncouth man

rucky down, crucky down stoop low, bend the knee

savise (savey, c.1785) know *'Do er want ter savise it?'* – 'Does he want to understand it?'

scarify (scarified, c.1541 – to scratch (in medical sense) c.1805 – to break up ground) to cultivate, scratch or scrape surface of soil to destroy weed, to talk angrily to someone *'I did scarify er, I did!'*

scat (c.1837) throw, cast, scatter, a scattering, a small amount; *'Scat un abroad'* – throw it about or break it in small pieces, *'Only a lill ol scat ov rain'* – a shower

scat abroad to go bankrupt

scoud to churn up *'They cows got into the gorden en scoud un up'*

scrawling (c.1380) fidgetting, shifting about on one's chair or seat

scriddick scrap, crumb, small amount of anything, a small almost worthless coin

scrud scab formed over a wound

scuffle (c.1798) farm implement for breaking down soil, a cultivator

scummer trouble, problem *'Us ad a propper ol scummer wi that job'*

shalder (c.1825) common yellow iris or flag

shammicks (shammock, c.1808) a poor lean animal

sherramooze shrew mouse

shippen, shippon (scypene, c.900) milking shed, a cow house

shrammed (shram, c.1787) to be cold

shug shy

skew-wiff askew, crooked in construction

skit diarrhoea (especially in calves)

skittery to be afflicted with diarrhoea

slay-roof sloping roof of lean-to building

slommick (slammakin, c.1785) untidy, slovenly, sloppy, dirty, (usually said of a female)

sloans, (slan, c.1000) sloe, sloes (fruit of blackthorn tree)

smeech, smitch (smec, c.825) smuts, small pieces of burnt material floating in air, smoke (particularly when it is not wanted such as in a room with a smoking chimney or in a garden affected by someone else's bonfire)

snooky (snoc-piece of land, c.1236) odd shaped piece of anything, particularly of a field

splits cut-rounds, baps

spuddle (c.1630) to move feebly *'Us found the ol cow,*

spuddlin bout on the ground and er couldn't get up'

squat (sqwat, c.1300) squashed *'Er trod on un, an squat un all abroad'*

stag (c.1730 – fighting cock of less than one year old) a cock bird amongst domestic hens

stap stop, visit *'Er's got zum ov they ol Frenchies* [French people] *stappin wi un'*

stape (c.1512) staple for fencing or holding wire

steep (c.1742) to layer a hedge (partially to cut through branches and bend them at the cut to re-make a worn or damaged hedge)

stent (stynte, c.1569) common ground, limit of right of pasturage on common land

stirrage (sterage, c.1513) commotion

stick (stikke, c.1386) handle of an implement such as a fork or hoe

sticks logs for burning, no matter how large

strabbly thin, scattered

strammer untruth

stroil (c.1758) couch grass *(Agropyrens ripens),* stubble

stromy streaky

stugged stuck, bogged down

succourable (socourabill, c.1400) sheltered, affording shelter

suent (suantly, c.1547) smooth (in all senses of the word) *'That went down suent!'* – said of something pleasant to eat or drink. *'It doant run suent like'* – something is not running smoothly

taffity (taffeta, c.1588) particular, dainty, fussy about food

tailpipe (c.1815) to tie a tin can to somebody else's dog's tail to frighten it off a farm (I know of a farmer who still does this!)

tallet (c.1586) loft above a building

tell (c.1864) talk, speak *'Wot be tellin bout you?'*

tempt touch *'Doant ee tempt it'* – 'don't touch it'

therle lean, gaunt, *'Er's so therle as a grey'ound'* – a poor sample [of grain]

thiggy, thicky that *thiggy rabbut* – that rabbit, *thicky thar* – that there.

thungy tough, doughy, like putty

tiddly goldfinch gold crested wren

tiddly, tiddly tope wren

tight arter close behind *'I went fust but Mother cum tight arter'*

till sow seed

tilth (tylthe, c.1496) soil broken down to a degree of fineness suitable for tilling

titmal, tittymal titmouse

titty-todger wren

tizzick sick, unwell in chest

toad riddings frogspawn

tom noddy tadpole *'Er's like a tomnoddy, all aid an no body'*

trapse (trappe, c.1400) walk without pleasure, drag one's feet wearily

trendle, trendow (trendyllys, c.1493) salting trough, trough for making dough, container for food. *'Nort in the trendow'* — nothing in the larder, no food available

trone up put grass or hay into wind-rows

tub (c.1602) gurnard

tuffs cut-rounds, baps

uff auver discuss, talk over a subject

up auver upstairs

ur he, it, (see *er* and section on grammar)

vady (c.1880) damp, musty *'The grass be too vady fer to siddown'*

vake rage, passion

vit dress meat, prepare it for cooking

vitty in good order

vitch polecat

vly-pecked low living, inferior thing or person

vores (c.1380) furrows

vore-edge, vorrage headland of field, part ploughed last

vrape, frape drawn tight, cut down

vrawed frozen

vreach violently

vuzkite kestrel

vuznapper, vuzchat whinchat

vuzzyvurze sweet chestnuts

wallage a large quantity *'Us've got wallages of grass'*

wangery soft, flabby

want (wond c.725) mole (animal)

want-heap mole-hill

Way! Stop! Woah! (command to horse or to human)

wester (westra, c.963) western

wetty damp, wet *'Tiz a bit wetty, you'* (raining hard!)

whippletree draught bar for pair or more of working horses

widder move about in nervous manner

widdywaddy stupidly weak, not to be relied upon

wildego naughty, unruly child

windle (c.1674) redwing, field-fare

winnard heron (this word appears in the OED but it is said to be a local word for a redwing. In my part of Devon, it is a grey heron)

winnet black cat with patch of white on backside

winnicky weak, inferior, small *'If you puts the bull to young yaffers, you'm only gwain ter get a winnicky lill ol calf, no good for nort'*

wipe (wype, c.1550) cut back, slash. Of an overgrown hedge *'Us'll wipe un off, you'*

wished (wish, c.1829) unhappy, miserable, pale

wished as a winnard miserable (as a grey heron looks when standing lonely on a river bank)

whistness melancholy

woppit (whapp, c.1440) box someone's ears *'Er geed un a woppit roun yurrole'*

wran (c.1450), **wranny** wren

wraxling (wraxlode, c.1000) wrestling

yamming jibbering, jabbering, outcry

yapping talking *'Us ad a good ol yap together'*, *'Us musn't stay yer yappin all day!'*

yark (c.1300) prepare, make ready, make haste

yawning, yamming lambing time

yaws ewes

yeth make haste

yeth ounds, zet ounds phantom pack of great hounds

yokey yellow, tawny-coloured

yucks hiccoughs

zamzawed tay tea stewed in the pot

zamzodden, zamsowden soft, daft, anything spoiled by being half cooked or overcooked

zamzoe, zamzod dough cake

zog doze *'I be gwain ter ave a bit of a zog'*

zourzobs sorrel (plant)

zowpeg woodlouse (see *chuggypig*)

zuft daft, soft

zugs bog, soft wet ground

Chapter 5

ETYMOLOGY

THE etymology of a word is its true original form and meaning. Far too many people, including those who should know better, tend to guess at the origins of words and fall into the trap of believing that one word is derived from another merely because it looks or sounds like it.

Having said this, the temptation to guess is almost irresistible. Earlier in this book I have told of the old lady who said that it was going to *blunk*. What is the origin of this word? I cannot find it in the OED and am sorely tempted to guess that it comes from the French *blanc*. On the other hand perhaps it is derived from the old French *blankete,* or indeed from some other word in some other language. I do not know the answer and doubt if I ever shall.

Hunting for the origins of words can become an addiction. The great Eric Partridge was a self-confessed addict of lexicography and John Moore once said that no one with the normal allowance of curiosity could look for a word in a dictionary without being diverted by the sight of another unconnected but unfamiliar word.

It is a pleasant and harmless addiction leading from the etymology of words to the meaning of place names, the origins of surnames and to the derivation of catch-phrases and slang.

In the pages which follow I have only attempted to produce the etymology of what I consider to be true dialect words. My information has been obtained from the Compact Edition of the OED. Every effort has been made to check their accuracy but I must accept full responsibility for any errors or omissions.

The etymology of Standard English words which are subjected to change by accent or pronunciation has not been included.

VOCABULARY

aneest (close to) The etymology of this word is not positive, either *ANEND* or *ANENT* from an old English phrase meaning on a level with. See also old English *NEAH* meaning nigh

angletitch (earthworm) This is rather nasty! It is a compound word. Old English *ANGUL*, meaning fish hook (only later line or tackle to which the hook was fastened), combined with old English *TWAECCA* which had the original sense of piercing or transfixing. Hence something that is transfixed on a hook – bait for fishing.

appledrain (wasp) Another compound. *APPLE* combined with old English *DRAN* meaning drone, male of honey bee or wasp

arrish (corn stubble) A particularly interesting word. Variant of *EDDISH* usually identified with old English *EDISC* a park or enclosure. The OED says that it is difficult to see

how the old English meaning could have given rise to the modern sense of the word. I do not agree; it is reasonable to relate stubble to an enclosed field because corn could only be grown successfully in an enclosed field which protected the crop from straying livestock.

axen (ashes), axwaddler Old English *ASCE,* old Norse *ASKA*

beastings (colostrum) Old English *BEOST.* Old High German, *BIOST;* the first milk drawn from a mammal, especially a cow after parturition.

beaufet (sideboard, cupboard) One of the words which shows how unwise it is to guess. One might (reasonably) imagine that it has something to do with good food. Not a bit of it! Middle French and middle English *BUFFET,* meaning a slap or blow. Diminutive of old French *BUFFE* (modern French *BAFFE*), a blow. Partridge records that

Bloch and Wartburg in their *Dictionnaire Etymologique de la langue Française* say 'Perhaps the word became the designation of a piece of furniture because the latter was originally furnished with a board that one could lower' – (presumably) with a smart tap or with the sound of a slap

belve (bellow) Middle English *BELWEN*. Old English *BELLAN*. Related to *BELCH* and *BELL*

ben (the truth) Middle English *BINNE*. Old English *BINNAN*, within, towards the inner part; by suggestion 'close to the truth of the matter'

billers (stem of plant) Believed to be from Middle English *BILLETTE*, a small round log; middle French *BILLART*, a staff, (hence *billiards*, a game played with a staff)

bird (girl) This is an interesting etymological roundabout. It is now considered to be rather racy to call a young woman a bird. It was not always thus. The word has come about by metathesis from the old English *BRID* and *BREDAN*, meaning nursling, something to cherish and keep warm, the young of either sex. It was once used in poetry to describe any lady but later was reserved only for young maidens, so was once respectable and even romantic, as it still is in dialect. A husband will say to his wife of whatever age 'Come on my burd, tiz time us was gwaine ome'

bist (are you, you are, you will be) Old Saxon *BIST* (Gospel according to St Luke, Chap.23.v.43 (c.1000) 'Today thou bist mid me on paridiso'.

bivver (tremble) Old English *BIFAN,* and old Saxon *BIVON,* to shake or tremble

blake (to faint, to turn pale) Middle Engwish *BLAKE,* shining, pale white, ultimately giving the modern word *bleach*

cater cousins (intimate friends) Johnson claimed that *CATER* came from the French *QUATRE* (four) used in the sense of a cousin, four times removed, he said 'from the ridiculousness of calling cousin or relation to so remote a degree'. There appears to be no etymological support for this suggestion and the OED suggests that it referred to persons treated as cousins because they were catered for within the household. It is to be found in Shakespeare (Merchant of Venice, Act II, scene 2) but I believe it still to be in use in dialectal speech. It was certainly used in writing in Devon in the early 19th cent.

chibbles (spring onions) French *CIBOULE,* and 3kanish *CEBOLLA,* a species of onion (*Allium fistulosum*) now rarely grown in England. It seems that the shoots of spring onions or young shallots look like this onion

chitterlings (pig's intestines cooked for human consumption) Old English, *CWITH,* womb. Chitterling is thought to be a distorted diminutive of this word. See also German

KUTTELN, tripe

chitterpie (magpie or human chatterbox) Onomatopoeic word; Dutch *KOETEREN* to jabber plus *PIE* which has an etymology which would fill pages. Latin *PICA* and Indo-European *PIK,* to pierce

chyney (things made of china material) Possibly from the CH'IN dynasty (255-206 BC). The OED says that China is not a Chinese word, but is found in Sanskrit about the time of the early Christian era, with modified forms elsewhere in Asia. Marco Polo referred to it as *CHIN* in 1516 and the material now called china is thought originally to have come from China

cladgy (waxy, sticky) Danish *KLAG, KLAGGE,* sticky mud, clay

clag, cleg (horsefly) Old Norse *KLEGGI,* modern Norwegian *KLEGG,* horsefly

claps (clasp or fasten) Middle English (by metathesis) *CLAPSEN,* also *clap* and *clip,* to fit together making a noise in so doing

clauvell (beam over fire place) French *CLAVEAU* keystone of arch, wedge-shaped lintel of window

clavel board, clavey board (mantelpiece) see above

clegged, clagged (animals fouled with their own dung) see *cladgy*

cloam (pottery clay) Old English *CLAM*, mud, clay

close (enclosure) Middle English from old French, *CLOS* and Latin *CLAUSUM*, an enclosure

coin (corner of house wall) Old French *COING*, an angle or corner, whence *COIGN*, wedge, stamp to mark precious metals used as money (coins)

courtiledge (farmyard) Old French *COURTILLAGE*, little court or garth, piece of ground attached to a dwelling house and forming one enclosure with it, or so regarded by the law. Now spelled curtillage and, outside dialect, mostly a legal term

crams (falsehoods) Old English *CRAMMIAN*, a derivative of *CRUMMEN*, meaning to insert, press or squeeze, to fill by force or compression. It appears to have become a slang word for lies (filling listeners with false information) in the late 1700s

crazed (in pain) Old French *ACRASER*, believed to be of Norse origin (Swedish KRASA, to crackle.) To break, to be broken, to be broken down in health. Thus crazy paving is not what it is generally supposed to be, a silly arrangement of stones, but paving made of broken and cracked stones. Similarly a crazy person is not just simple but broken in his mind

cubbert (cupboard) A combination of two words, Old English *CUPPE*, a drinking vessel and Old Saxon *BORT*, meaning a board, shelf, or trencher. The combination of the two words remained until the 18th cent. when *cubbert* was the common spelling and presumably the normal pronunciation. It survives only in dialect

culver (pigeon) Old English *CULFRE* from Latin *COLUMBA* dove or pigeon

curious (careful) Old French *CURIUS,* a word with many shades of meaning but originally giving care, being careful, studious or attentive. See also Latin *CURA,* anxiety, care, medical care, to cure

dewsnail (slug) Old English *DEAW,* old Saxon *DAW,* to flow, run (dew was formerly believed to flow from the heavens), plus old English *SNAEGL,* snail or slug

dimmity, dimmit, dimps (twilight) Derivatives of old English *DIM,* obscure, dim, dark

ditch (a bank) Old English *DIC,* which has also given us dyke. It originally meant channel, deep furrow, excavation, but came to mean the earth thrown up as a result of digging the channel

doilish (in one's dotage) Old English *DOL,* dull, stupid, foolish, particularly when such failings were caused by old age

drade (material, substance) Local pronunciation of *trade,* Old English

TREDAN, to tramp, to follow a path for the purpose of commerce, thence goods bought or sold, finally any goods or substance

drags (harrows) Old English *DRAGAN,* to trail anything along the ground or on other surface where there is friction or resistance

drangway (narrow lane) Variant of *DRONG,* old English *RINGAN,* to press, compress (thence a passage way through which one presses one's way) Modern German *DRINGEN* to press forward, to penetrate. (This is one of the many words about which guesses have been made – a *draying way* along which goods are drawn (see *dray*) but this guess is far from the truth)

dray (carry a load) Old English *DRAGAN,* to draw, originally a sled or something for dragging turf, wood, etc. The word draw as in drawing a picture is from the same root in the sense that the pencil is dragged across the paper. It also gives us the action of extracting something, drawing a tooth, drawing water or drawing the dole. In Devonshire we *dray* a photograph

drecksill (doorstep) a compound word, German, *DRECK,* mud, filth, and middle English *SYLLE,* the base of a frame

drumbledrane (bumble- bee) another compound. Old English *DUMB* meaning mute or stupid, plus old English *DRAN,* to resound or boom. The word therefore suggests a lazy insect that makes a loud noise – a little unfair I think to the attractive bumblebee. The etymology of bumblebee is interesting and worth recording in this context. Middle English, *HUMBLE-BEE,* an insect which hums. Nothing to do with being humble

dryth (degree of dryness) Old English *DRYGE,* to be dry

durn (door frame) Old Swedish *DYRNI,* Norwegian *DYRN,* a door

eaver (rye grass) French

IVRAIE VIVACE, ryegrass

evil (shovel) Old English *GEAFUL,* a fork. Alternative form is *GIFEL* which has become *evil* by local pronunciation. Quite how a fork became a shovel is not clear; possibly any implement used to shove or push

fancical (strange) Late Middle English *FANCY,* a contraction of *FANTASY* which comes to us from old French *FANTASIE* deriving from Latin and Greek words meaning figures of the imagination, phantom

ferry, fairy, vairy, vaire (weasel) Old French *VAIR,* Latin *VARIUS,* partly coloured. Orginally fur obtained from a variety of squirrel with a grey back and white belly, much used for trimming garments (as was ermine). It seems that Cinderella's slipper was not made of glass (French *verre*) but of fur (French *vair*), a much more likely material

fitch (polecat, ferret) Old French *FISSEL*

frape (tie tightly, cut down

closely) Old English
(GE)FRAEPGIGA old
French *FRAPER,* to
strike, to beat, to bind
tightly, to brace the cords
of a drum by pulling
them together

galley (frighten) Old
English *A-GAELWAN,* to
alarm

gambers (hocks of animal,
ankles of human) Old
French *GAMBE,* the leg
of an animal represented
in heraldic design. See
also Italian *viola da gamba*
a viola held between the
legs as compared with the
viola da braccio, an
instrument held in the
arms. Also modern
French *JAMBE,* leg

glint (peep, look shyly)
Middle English *GOLET,*
throat, old French
GOULET, GOLE and
GOULE, throat, see also
gurgle and gullet

golden gladdi
(yellowhammer) Old
English *GLAED,* bright,
joyous

grab (crab apple) Swedish
SKRABBA, the fruit of
wild apple tree

gulch (to swallow) Swedish
dialect *GOLKA,* German
dialect, *GULKEN,* to
swallow greedily

havage (ancestry) The verb
to have derives through
middle English *HAVEN*
or *HABBEN* and old
English *HABBAN,* to
hold or to take. The
suffix age comes from old
French which has
numerous meanings but
includes a collective
sense. *Havage* simply
means the holding of
something collective, such
as ancestry, lineage or
parentage

having (behaviour)
(rhymes with shaving)
French *AVOIR,* to have.
14th and 15th cent. variants
give the sense of behaviour,
bearing, manner

heft (weigh) Old English
HEBBAN, to move up, to
move along, to lift (via
modern English *HEAVE*)

hogs (yearling sheep) A
very interesting word.
Old English *HAGG,*
possibly of Celtic origin.
The OED suggests that
the word may originally
have had reference to the
age of the beast. The
yearling age group runs
through the use of this
word when applied to
both sheep and pigs

ile (awn on barley) Old
English *EGLE* or
EIGLE original Teutonic
AGLI. The OED quotes
an early version of the
Gospel according to St
Luke, Chap.6,v.41,
which when translated
into modern English,
reads, 'why see'st thou
the barley-awn in thy
brother's eye?'

ire (iron) Here is a word
which has undergone
many changes. Old
English *IREN* which in
middle English became
IRE. The etymology is
probably Norse.
Partridge relates the word
ORE to the old English
AR meaning copper,
brass, or metal. The
middle English version is
retained in Devon
dialects and is in daily
use in the compound
BAR-IRE meaning a
crow-bar. The expressive,
'It were freezin bar-ires'
is used to describe very
cold weather

**kickshaw (useless
ornament, pretty trifle)**
French *QUELQUE
CHOSE* shortened to
QUE'QUE CHOSE,
something, thing-a-me-bob

**lade (load, ladder like
fixture on cart)** Old
English *HLAED*, a
stack, pile, load. When
used in the context of a
cart fixture, something
which increases the
capacity to carry a load.
Survives in standard
English in the word
LADEN

leary (empty) Old English
LAERE, empty

leat (conduit) Old English
WAETER GELIET, a
water conduit

leer (flank of man or beast)
Old English *LIRA*, the
fleshy part of the body

lern (teach) A fine example
of the use of a word in
dialect which is now
regarded as being
incorrect. Old English
LAERAN, Middle
English *LERNEN*, to
teach. Etymologically, the
word teach means to
show or guide, and the
fact that one *learns* by
being *taught* has been
confused in common
usage. The dialect 'I'll
lern ee' meaning 'I will
teach you' is not
incorrect

linney (lean-to shed) Old
English *HLINIAN*, to
lean. A shed or farm

building with open front
and lean-to roof. Some-
times spelled linhay, but,
contrary to some guess-
work etymology, has
nothing to do with hay

main (powerful) Old Norse
MEGN, strong, powerful
maunchuss see *main*
maund (basket) Old
English *MAND,* basket
made of wicker or some
other woven material
mawses, morses (roots of
trees or plants) Old
English *MORE,* a root of
tree
mind (remember) Old
English *MUNAN,* to
think, to remember
mommet (scarecrow) Old
French *MAHUMET,* an
idol, (from false medieval
notion that the prophet
Mohammed was
worshipped)
moor (unproductive land)
Old English *MOR,* a
moor. Akin to old
English *MERSC* a marsh,
from Latin *MARE,* the
sea
moowey (rickyard) Old
English *MUHA,* old
Norse *MUGE,* a swath,
stack of hay, a heap of
hay or grain in a barn
mort (a lot) Possibly old

Norse *MART,* great, a
great number, but this is
not certain. More likely
French *MORTIE,*
something (so big) that it
frightens one to death
mun (them) Old English
MANNIAN, a person

nammet (mid-morning
snack) Variation of
NUMMET, a corruption
of *NOON-MEAT*
niddick (nape of neck) Old
English *HNECCA*

obbledehoy (term of
disdain) Middle English
HOBBLE, to move with
clumsy gait
orts (remains of food,
refuse) Not in general use
until the end of 16th
cent., possibly from
Dutch *OOR-AETE,* the
remains of food, left-ōvers

paunched, poached (land
damaged by over-
stocking) Related to
words *POKE, POACH*
and *POACHER,* to thrust
or dig out with fingers.
Old English *POHHA,*
pocket, Modern French
POCHE, a pocket or
pouch. Hence land that is
full of pockets of water
and mud

pick (pitchfork) Old French *PIC,* English *PIKE,* a foot soldier's weapon. A pitchfork is very like a pike (and indeed was used as such as recently as the 1940s when the LDV, later the Home Guard, initially had no better weapons than pitchforks.)

pinswill (a small boil) Etymology uncertain but probably old English *PINN* a pin, peg, point (a boil or swelling rises to a point). It also feels perhaps like the pricking of a pin

ploo (plough) Old English *PLOH*

pook (haycock) Old English *POCC,* French *POCHE,* a gathering together, a pocket, see *paunched* above. All these words have the same root

popples (pebbles) An interesting word. Old English *PAPOLSTANAS* probably onomatopoeic and said to be the noise made by water running over stones

power (a number) Middle English *POER,* mastery or power. A large enough number to be powerful. See modern mathematical usage, 'x to the power of three'

prang (hayfork) Middle English *PRANGE,* variation of *PRONGE,* a sharp pain, hence tine of fork which can inflict such a pain. Modern English *PRONG.* (A *prang* is a hayfork with two prongs, but a *pair of prangs* is a dung fork with four prongs)

prize (a fulcrum) Old French *PRISE,* taking, seizing, capturing. Connected with modern English, *APPREHEND.* Modern English usage 'to prize open'

pug (sea trout) Etymology uncertain but word appears to refer to the size of the fish since it is also used to describe an elf, a small dog, a small lamb and other small things. A *pug* was probably regarded as a small salmon, although this is of course incorrect

quarrel (pane of glass) Middle English *QUAREL,* a square. Thus the word relates to the shape of the pane, and not to the material from which it is made

quoin (a corner) see *coin* above

rabin urdick (Robin redbreast) *Rabin* is simply a dialectal form of Robin, a pet name for Robert, but *urdick* is most interesting. *URD* is red having undergone metathesis, and *dick* was an early 19th cent. word for a leather apron, a worn-out shirt. Hence a covering worn to protect the front of one's dress during work – Robin red apron/shirt/dicky/breast

raymes (skeleton, remains) Old high German *RAMA*, modern German *RAHM*, a ramework, the bones or skeleton of a human or animal. In dialect it is used in the context of something left over 'Missus give me the raymes of a rabbut pie fer me dinner'

revel (merrymaking) (One still speaks of the 'Clovelly Revels', an annual sports-day/fête raising funds for Church and Parish Hall). Old French *REVEL*, a revolt, din, disorder – hence the noise of merry-making

rigmarole (a lot of talk or fuss, a long letter or document) Middle English *RAGEMAN*, a state or Papal document, esp. of an Act passed in 1276 by King Edward I for the hearing of ancient wrongs. This became *RAGMAN*, and *RAGMAN-ROLLS* were deeds written on parchment on which, in 1291 and 1293, Scottish Lords and gentlemen swore allegiance to the King of England

savise (to know, to understand) French *SAVOIR* – *SAVEZ VOUS*, 'Do you know?'

scarify (to scratch surface) Middle French *SCARIFIER*, from Latin *SCARIFICARE*, to scratch

scat (scatter etc.) Middle English *SCATEREN*, to split up, to strew about

scrawling (shifting in one's seat, fidgeting) A form of *CRAWL*, perhaps suggested by *SPRAWL*, old English *SPREAWLIAN*. To move in ungainly or awkward manner

scuffle (a cultivating implement) Dutch

SCHOFFEL, a weeding hoe

shippen (a milking shed) Old English *SCYPEN,* a shed

shrammed (to be cold) Old English *SCRIMMAN,* to be paralysed with the cold

sloans (fruit of blackthorn, sloe, sloes) Old English *SLA* (plural *SLAN*) This plural usage was recorded in the 17th cent. It is retained in Devon dialect but is given an additional plural ending s. I have never heard it used in the singular

smeech (smuts, smoke) Old English *SMEC,* smoke, dense or thick vapour

snooky (odd shaped piece of something) From the standard English *NOOK,* middle English *NOK,* a nook, corner, angle

squat (squashed) Old French *ESQUATIR,* to crush, flatten, beat out of shape, smash, squash, bruise

stag (a cock bird) another word which refers to the sex of the subject. Old English *STAGGA,* old Norse *STEGGI,* a male bird. In modern usage, a male deer

stape (a staple) Old English *STAPOL,* a post, pillar, step, a looped device from which to hang merchandise in a market place. Middle English *ESTAPLE,* a mart

steep (to layer a hedge) Old English *STUPIAN,* to stoop down, to bow, hence to bend down branches of saplings to make a hedge

stent (common land boundry) Old French *ESTENTE,* meaning extent – the limitation on freedom of pasturage on common land

stirrage (commotion) Old English *STYRIAN,* to disturb

stick (wooden handle of hoe or fork) Old English *STICCA,* to pierce, a pointed instrument, a rod with which to pierce or poke, a piece of wood shaped for a purpose

succourable (sheltered) Old French *SO-SUCURABLE,* affording succour, helpful. Modern French *SECOURS,* relief, aid

suent (smooth) old French *SUIANT,* modern French *SUIVRE,* to follow, thus to proceed smoothly, evenly

taffity (dainty) Old French *TAFFETAS*, silken cloth, hence something attractive, dainty

tallet (a loft) French *TABULARE*, floor-boarding. (A tallet is a loft formed by laying boards over the rafters of a cattle shed or stable)

tell (talk, speak) Old English *TELLAN*, what one has to tell, to talk about

tellan (speaking) see above 'I doant knaw wot you be tellan bout!'

tempt (to touch) Middle English *TEMPTEN* from Latin *TEMPTARE*, to touch

tilth (soil sufficiently broken down for sowing seed) Old English *EORTHTILTH*, labour involved in cultivation, tillage, husbandry

trendle (salting trough) Old English *TRENDEL*, a circle or ring, a vessel of flat and rounded form, a circular trough or tray used by bakers

vores (furrows) Old English *FURH*, middle Dutch *VOOR*, a narrow trench made in the earth for drainage purposes, or to receive seed at planting time

want (mole) Old English *WAND* or *WOND*, mole or shrew

wester (western) Old English *WESTRA*, lying towards the west

wipe (to cut or slash) Old English *WIPIAN*, to wind around, to whip, to slash

wran (wren) Old English *WRENNA* or *WERNA*

wraxling, wrassling (wrestling) Old English *WRAXLIAN*, to wrestle, strive, contend

yamming (jibbering) Middle Dutch *JAMMER* (pronounced yammer) a loud outcry

yark (to make ready) Old English *GEARCIAN*, to prepare, make ready

Chapter 6

VOCABULARY

THIS vocabulary consists of standard English words and their equivalents in local pronunciation or in dialect.

abcess aps, pinswill
about bouta
above abew, upauver
account counton
afraid aveered, feared, veered
after arter
after all avore-all
against agin, genst, gin, ginst (hard G)
ailing pinking
alder (tree) aller
Alfie, Alfred Aufy, Offy
Alice Else
alight (from something) onlight
alms ormers
always awiz, orwiz
amazed maized, mazed
am not ant
ancestry havage
andiron viredog
angle ango
angle-iron ango-ire
ankles gambers
anointed nointed
another anither
anxious angshus
anything aut, awt
apron apern
argue argify, argy
ashes axen

ask ax
asked axed
askew skew-whiff
attacked attack-ted
audacious owdacious
aught ort
awkward ockard
awn (of barley) barleyzears, ile

baby babby
baby boy biye
baby girl cheel
back-kitchen backouze, back-house
backwards assards, backzivore
bankrupt (to go) go scat, go squat
bark (like small dog) yap
barley awns barleyzears
barrel barriole
bawl baal
beam (over fireplace) clauvel
bean bain
beastly bissle
beasts baistzez
beautiful britiful, bootiful
beauty booty
because cos, cuz, vor-why
bed baid

beef baive, beeve
been bain, bin
beer bair
beetle biddle
before avore, be-vower, vaur, vor
before daylight vaurday
behave being-have (rhymes with shave)
bellow belve
bellows bellerziz
belly-band bellybon
besides azides
bequest bequath
bewitched begayed
bigoted bigotive
bird baird, bard, burd
biscuit bisky
blackbird blackdrish
bleed blaid
blindfold bline-mop
blisters bladders
blood blid
bloom bloath, bloo, blooth
blossom blooth
bluebells goocoos
bogged down stugged
bogs zugs
boil bile
boiling bile-in
borrow borry
bottle boddle
boy biye, bye
brambles brimbles, brimmles
bread braid
breakfast braxis, braxus, brexis
breeches burches

bridge burge
bronchitis brantitis, browntitus
brook (artifical) leat
brother brither
brother-in-law brither-en-law
bruised brit
brush brish
bull bool, bule
bullfinch hoop
bumblebee drumbledrane, umble
burst bost, bust
business bizzens
butchering butchin
by-and-by bimeby

candle cannel
candlelight cannel teening
cannot cas'n
careful curious
carpenter cafender
cart (carry) dray
case cause, caze
cast (scatter) scat
cat (female) yaw-cat
catch ketch
caterpillar (esp. Cabbage White) mascall
celebration frawzey
certain zartain
chaffinch (cockbird only) copperfinch
challenge channis
chamber chimber
cheek chack
chestnuts (sweet) vuzzyvurze

child cheel
chimney chimbley, chimley
china (material) chyney
chit chid
chore chewer
clasp claps
clay (object made of clay)
   cloam, cloamen
clerk clurk
clever cliver
climb climey
clod clat
close (to, by) tight-arter
clothes claws
cloudy owdry
clover-hay cloveray
club-foot pimple-voot
coarse coose
coat caw-at
cock bird stag
cold (to be) shrammed
collection (of something)
   passel
colostrom beastings, bizzy-
   milk
comfortable con-for-able
common-ground stent
commotion stirrage
confused confuddled
confusion mizmaze
consequence konsekense
contemptible shitten
continue continny
cor! (exclamation) gaw!
corner coin, cornder,
   (corner of building, wall),
   quoin
correct cracked, krackt
couch grass stroil

crab apple grab
cranefly (daddy-longlegs)
   granfer-longlaigs
cream craim
creak crake
crooked crumpety
crop crap
crow-bar bar-ire
crumb crub
cultivate (the soil) scarify
cupboard cubbert
cupboard (glass-fronted)
   beaufet
curlygreens (vegetable)
   crilly-grains
cut (back, down) frape,
   vrape, wipe-off

daffodils (wild) lent lilies,
   lenten roses
daft mazed, zamsowden,
   zamzodden, zuft
dainty taffity
damp vady
dandruff scruff
daren't durzant
daughter darter
dead daid
deaf deef, deave
deal (wood) dell
dearly dairly
deceit dezait
deceive dezaive
delay hinderment
depth deepth
devil dowel
Devon Dabn, Debn, Demshur
diarrhoea (esp. in animals)
   skit

die dee
directly drackly
dirty bissle, shitten
discuss uff-auver
doesn't dith'n, doth'n
dog dug
done, did dood
don't know dannaw, disn't naw
doorframe durn, durnaid, durndle
doorstep, threshold drecksill, dreckstool, druckssool
dotage doilish
doze zog
dragonfly horse-long-cripple
draw (carry, cart, take) dray
dried adrowed
drive draive, draw
drove drauved
dust brist, mux-adrowed, pillum
duster dister

each aich
ear yer, yur, yurole
earth ay-uth
earthworm angletitch, angletwitch
eastern easter
easy aizy
eat ait, ate
eel ail
eggs aigs
either aither
elephant huffilant

eleven lebn, lem
else alse, ulse
empty empt (to empty) leary (to be empty)
end aend, ayend
engine injin
enough nuff
entertainment intertainment
equal aikel
errand arrant
eternal tarnal
evening ayve-mun, aivmin, evelings
ewe yaw
exactly zackly

faith feth, fey
fall vahl, vall
far var
farmer varmer
farming varmering
farm-yard curtiledge
farther varder
farthest vardist
fast vast
fault vot
features (looks) vaityers
fen venn
ferret fitch
field-fare windle
fierce brinded
fire avire
fire-dog viredug
fish vish
fit, fitting vitty
flabby wangery
flank leer
floorboards planchin

fool vule
forewarning voretoken
foxglove cowflop, floppy-dock
frighten frit, galley
frightened aveered
frogspawn toadriddings
from vrim
front furnt
frozen vrawed
furrows vores
furze vuzz
fuss (commotion) pucker, stirrage

gate ge-at
gate hook (fastening on gate) ge-at ook
getting along, getting on nackin vore
giggle siggle
gin jean
girl (baby) cheel
give gee
glance (peep) glint
glass (something made of) glassen
glowering glousing
goes goeth, go'th
going gain, gwain
goose guze
gooseberry goosegog
gorse chad, chag, fuzz, vuzz
gossip croosle
guinea fowl glinney
gulley goil
gurnard (fish) tub
grandfather gonmer,

granfer, grampy
grandmother gonmer, grammar
gravel grovel
greased graized
great (large) gurt, master, maunchuss
greedy gutsing
green grin

habit (conduct) gyte
hair ayer
halfpenny apmee
hames aimzes
handkerchief ankcher
handsome ansum, bowerly
happen apn
harken arken
harrows (spike) drags
hasp apse
haste (make haste) yeth
haul all
have hab
have not abn, habn
hawk (any bird of prey) kit
haycock pook
hazel bushes nittals
he er, ur, ee
head aid
headland (of field) vore-edge, vorrage
hear yur
heat yet
heath yeth
heating yettin
heave ay-ve
heifer yaffer
heinous hengous
hedge ay-je

hedgehog ay-je-boar
hedge trough (ditch) ay-je-draw
herbs arbs, yarbs
here yur, yer
heron harnzee, winnard
hey-ho! hey-go!
hiccough yucks
hill eel
hindrance hinderment
hit clump, dap
hoard wurd
hocks gambers
hold holt
holiday-maker grockle
holler holley
honey bay-spittal
hook ook
hope awp, awps
horsefly clag, cleg
however owsom-iver
huge laceing, maunchuss
hungry grubbish, leery, ungered
hurry chur
hut orted

icicles chonchables
idiot idjit
ignorant iggerent
impertinence himperence
impossible onpossible
improper onproper
impudence himperence
in een
indecency ondaicentness
indecent ondaicent
inferior (in size) winnicky
inflammation infermation

injured orted
interfere (meddle) meel
intestines natlings
inwards (inward parts) innards
iron ire
irregular onwriggler

jackdaw chauk
jolt jolk
judge jidge
jumble-sale jumbo-zale

kale caul
kestrel vuz-kite
key kay
kite kit
knew nawed
knocked nacked
know savis

laden lade
lapwing hornywink
large bowerly, gurt, hengous, laceing (something large – a lacer)
later bimeby
lath (as in lath & plaster) laff
laughed laffed
launch laanch
lean lain, therle
learn larn
leave laive
lee (sheltered from wind) lew, loo
leg laig
listen arken

litter (rubbish) louster
little leel, leet
load law
loan lent
loft tallet
logs sticks
look! (see!) lookee!
losing losting
lover luvver

maintain forestain
man mun
marbles aggets, marvels
market margit, morket
marshes mashes, moors
masonry (working as a
  mason) masony
mister maister
mattock doobail, fisgie,
  maddock
mean nair
meddle meel
melancholy whistness
mice meeze
might (power) me-art
mildewed moundery
milk (to milk) mulkee
miserable wisht
misslethrush homescreech
mole want
molehill mole heave, want
  heap, want heave
monkey mokus
moor (wet, unproductive
  land) ma-ur
morning vorenoon
moss mauth, mose
mould moulder
muck mux

mucky, muddy muxy
mushroom mushelroom
musty peendy

nape of neck niddick
naught nort
naughts and crosses
  aughts'n crosses
naughty child lill heller,
  wildego
near (mean) nair
neither nother
never niver
none noan
nonsense (to talk n.)
  blinemares
northern norther
nose nawse
nothing nort
notice nawtiz

oats wuts
officer hossifer
old aud
old woman (wife)
  o-dumman
one another one tother
open ope
otherwise else
ought ort
oven omm
over awver
overthrow auverdraw
owned awned

package passel
painful crazed
pale blake, palled, wisht
pane of glass quarrel

party (celebration) frawzey
passion (anger) vake
panting pankin
particular taffity
parcel passel
parson passen
particularly purtickly
partridge paltridge
passageway (narrow)
   drangway
peace paice
pebble popple, popplestone
peep (look shyly) glint
perfection purveckshun
photograph votee
piece paice
pig peg
pigeon culver
pigsty pegslooze
pillow peel
pillowcase peel-bears
pitching (throwing) pitchin
pity pittis
pixy piskie, pisky
planking (floorboards)
   planchin
plenty hundreds
plot (of land) plat
plough ploo
poison powsen
pole pool
polecat fitch, vitch
poor pawer
polyanthus polyanties
post (stake) pauss
posts posses, postses
potato tater, teddy, tiddy
pour pawer
prepare (make ready) yark

pretend make wise
primrose pimrose,
   primrosen
print pernt
prong prang
proper prapper, vitty
pull (draw) dray
puzzled flummoxed

quantity (of something)
   passel
quay kay
queen cat yaw cat
queer que-ar
quiet kwai-it

rage vake
rattle rittle
raw rare
reach raich
red urd
redwing windle
remains orts, rames
remember mind
revel (jollification, fête) rail
ribbons erbons, urbons
rich urch
Richard Urchard
rickyard moowey, mow,
   mowhay
ridiculous re-dicklus
road raud, rawed
robin redbreast rabin
   urdick
roots (of tree or plant)
   mawses, mores
rotted ratted
roughcast rowcast
row raw

royal rile
rubbish rummage
run rin
runt (smallest pig) chuggy-
    pig, nissledraft
rut rout
rusty risty

salt zalt
sand zand
sap zap
saucy sassy
scarecrow mommet
scatter scat, zlatter
scheme gyte, scheemy
scholar scollard
scurf scruff
sect sex, zext
sell zill
several sivver
shabby (trick) scabby
shale (sedimentary rock)
    shillet
sheep shape, yaws
shelter (from wind)
    lewness, lewth
sheltered side lewzide,
    succorable
shitty (dirty) shitten
shout holly
shoot shet
shovel evil, shoel, showel
show (exhibition) shaw
shred shreed
shriek scritch
shut shet
shy shug
sick tizzick
sieve zaive

sigh sife, sify
simple-minded zauney
skewer skivver
skin skeen
slam stram
sloe slome, (sloans)
smallest smarless
smooth suent
snack (elevenses) nammett
sneeze neeze
snowing blunkin
sow (seed) till
speed chur
squeeze creem
staple (fastening) stape
stonechat fuzzchat
stormy (sky) stromy
streaky stromy
stuck (bogged down)
    stugged
soft (flabby) wangery,
    zamzodden
soil ay-uth
soldier sauger, sodger,
    solger, sudger
something zummat
sooner (rather) zoonder
soul zaw
southern souther
speak spake
speckled spekerty
spectacles spurticles
squash squat
squat quot, quat
squeamish skimmish
started starded
staunch staint
stay bide
sticky kaky, clitchy

stinks stanks
stoat blacktail
stolen stauld
stove bodley, stauve
stoop steep
struggling spuddling
stubble arrish
stuck stugged
stump stub
stupid stoopid
suffocated buddled
sure zartain, zhure
sun zin
swallow (consume) gulch
swath (of grass) zwar, zwaur
sweltering quelstring

tadpole blackaid, tomnoddy
talk tell
talking yabbing, yappin
tantrum flicket
tap (hit) dap
tarpaulin haler
tasks chewers
tea tay
teach larn
tear (break) tar
tease (wool) toze
tease (annoy) terrify
tedious tayjess
thatching datchin
thaw (to thaw something) onthaw
them mun
thin strabbly
thing item
thirteen dirteen
thistle dashel

thrash drash
three dree
throat drot
throw ay-ve, scat
throwing pitchin
thrown drowed, drawed
throw up (vomit, refer back) draw-up
thrush drish, drishel, greybird
thump clump
tight-fisted nair
titmouse hickymal, titmal, tittymal
titter siggle
toad taw'd
tom-tit bloath-pecker
touch tempt
tough thungy
towards genst (hard G)
tremble biver
trial (in court) yurrin
trick gyte
tread trade
tremendous hengous
trough draw, traw, trow
true jonnick
two doo

uncivil ondaicent
uncomfortable oncomforable
uncover onhale
understand savis
undress onwray
uneven onwriggler
unknowing onnawin
unpunctual onwriggler
untruth strammer

unwell pluff
upon pun
upset upzot
upstairs upauver

value valley
vehicles vay-acles
veterinary vetinry
vermin varmint
victuals vittles
visitor (holidaymaker) grockle
violently vreach

wager wajer
walk (wearily) trapse
wallowing walvin
walnut frenchnut
warrant waarn
wasp appledrain, apple-drone, wapsie, wopsie
weak wick
weasel ferry, fairy, vair, vairy
weather ware, wur
wedge waj
weigh heft
western wester
whet (sharpen) wad
whitlow nimpingang
wicked nointed
wife wive
William Wi-yum
winchat vuznapper, vuzchat
witfbway
within way-een
without uthout
woman ooman, dumman

wood ood
woodlouse (North Devon dialect) chuggypig
woodpecker oodwall
world ay-uth, wurdle
worm angledog, angletwich
would wude
wren crackety, cracky-wran, kracketty, tiddly tope, titty todger, wran, wranny
wrestling wraxling

yellowhammer golden gladdi, gladdy
yellow (coloured) yokey
yes ace, ees, iss
yourself yerzel

Zed (the letter) zad

BIBLIOGRAPHY

THIS bibliography lists some of the works consulted in dealing with this subject. Publication dates are those of the editions used by the author.

AUSTEN, JANE: *Persuasion* (first published 1818). London; Dent, 1906 Everyman's Library. New York; Dutton, 1906.

BARZUN, JACQUES & GRAFF HENRY.F: *The Modern Researcher*. New York, Chicago, San Francisco, Atlanta; Harcourt, Brace & World Inc., 1970.

BAUGH, ALBERT.C & CABLE, THOMAS: *A History of the English Language*. London; Routledge and Kegan Paul, 1951.

BOWRING, SIR JOHN: *Language with special reference to the Devonshire Dialects*. Report and Transactions of the Devonshire Association, 1866.

CHOPE, R, PEARSE. *The Dialect of Hartland, Devonshire*. London; Kegan Paul, Trench, Trubner, 1891.

COBBETT, WILLIAM. *Rural Rides*. London; J.M. Dent & Sons Ltd, Everyman's Library, 1912, reprinted 1966.

COLES, ALBERT, J. *Ole Biskit*. London; Herbert Jenkins, 1933. *A Parcel of ol' Crams*. Gloucester; Alan Sutton Publishing Limited, 1980. (First published 1930, republished 1980 by arrangement with the copyright holders).

CRYSTAL, DAVID (ed) *Eric Partridge, in his own words*. London; André Deutsch, 1980.

DEVONSHIRE ASSOCIATION FOR THE ADVANCEMENT OF SCIENCE, LITERATURE AND ART, *Report and Transactions, 1877*. (This particular volume contains the terms of reference of the committee established to record Devonshire provincialisms, and for this reason has been singled out. All annual reports and transactions since that date contain reference to dialect).

EKWALL, EILERT. *The Concise Oxford Dictionary of English Place Names*. Oxford University Press, 1936; 2nd edn, 1940; 3rd edn, 1947; 4th edn, 1960, reprinted 1950, 1964, 1966, 1970 and 1974.

ELWORTHY, FREDERICK THOMAS, *The Dialect of West Somerset*, London; Trubner, 1875-86. (This volume contains three works, originally presented as individual papers: (i) *'The Dialect of West Somerset'*, (ii) *'Grammar of West Somerset Dialect'*, and (iii) *'West Somerset word-book or Glossary'*.

GWATKIN Mrs (ed), *A Devonshire Dialogue in Four Parts* Plymouth; Edward Nettleton, 1839. London; G.B. Whittaker, 1839.

HALLIWELL, JAMES ORCHARD, *Dictionary of Archaisms and Provincialisms*. London; George Routledge and Sons, 1904. New York, E.P. Dutton & Co. 1904.

HEWETT, SARAH, *The Peasant Speech of Devon*. London; Elliott Stock, 1892.

HOLE, THE REVEREND WILLIAM, *The Exmoor Scolding and Courtship*. London; *The Gentleman's Magazine*, 1746.

JENNINGS, JAMES KNIGHT, *The Dialect of the West of England*. London; John Russell Smith, 1869.

MARTIN, E. W. *The Secret People*. London; Phoenix House Ltd, 1954. New York; Transatlantic, 1956. *The Shearers and the Shorn*, London; Routledge & Kegan Paul. New York; 1965, Humanities Press, 1965.

McADAM, Jr E. L. & MILNE, GEORGE. *Johnson's Dictionary, a Modern Selection*. London; Book Club Associates, by arrangement with Victor Gollancz Ltd, 1982.

MOORE, JOHN. *You English Words*. London; Collins, 1961.

ORTON, H and others (ed), *Survey of English Dialects* (1961-72). E. J. Arnold. *The Linguistic Atlas of England*. Croom Helm, 1978.

OXFORD ENGLISH DICTIONARY, *Compact Edition*. Oxford University Press, 1971, Book Club Associates, 1979. (This is the complete text of the 1933 re-issue, reproduced micrographically, condensing twelve volumes into only two).

PARTRIDGE, ERIC. *A Dictionary of Slang and Unconventional English*. London; Routledge, 1937. *Usage and Abusage: A Guide to Good English*. New York; Harper, 1942. (1st British edition, revised and enlarged, London; Hamilton, 1947). *Origins: A Short Etymological Dictionary of Modern English*. London; Routledge and Kegan Paul, 1958. *The Gentle Art of Lexicography, as pursued and Experienced by an Addict: A Memoir.* London; André Deutsch, 1963.

PHILLIPS, THE REVEREND JOHN. *Glossary to the Devonshire Dialogue in Four Parts.* Plymouth; Edward Nettleton, 1839. London; G.B. Whittaker, 1839.

TREVELYAN, G.M. *English Social History.* London; Longmans Green, 1944.

ENDPIECE

HAD it not been for Eric Partridge, I doubt if I would ever have attempted to write this book. I will end it by quoting him:

'It is to be hoped that dialect-speakers will not be shamed out of their words, phrases, and pronunciations by "cultured" visitors, by near-visioned teachers, by B.B.C. "experts". The influence of "education" is already visible in the weakening of the local pronunciation of Circencester (Sissiter), Bodiam, (Bodjum), Daventry (Danetree), Yealm (Yam): it is time that the curb and snaffle of good sense should put a check to the nefarious teachings of the unimaginatively genteel. Country people are too modest. They must sturdily resist the insidious approaches of their "betters". They should boldly preserve the traditional pronunciations.' *(Usage and Abusage)*